THE BEST OF

CORWIN

EDUCATIONAL NEUROSCIENCE

The Best of Corwin Series

Classroom Management
Jane Bluestein, Editor

Differentiated Instruction
Gayle H. Gregory, Editor

Differentiated Instruction in Literacy, Math, and Science
Leslie Laud, Editor

Educational Neuroscience
David A. Sousa, Editor

Educational Technology for School Leaders
Lynne M. Schrum, Editor

Equity
Randall B. Lindsey, Editor

Inclusive Practices
Toby J. Karten, Editor

Response to Intervention
Cara F. Shores, Editor

THE BEST OF CORWIN

EDUCATIONAL NEUROSCIENCE

DAVID A. SOUSA
Editor

With contributions by

David A. Sousa ▪ Robert Sylwester ▪ Sheryl G. Feinstein

Pamela Nevills ▪ Abigail Norfleet James ▪ Eric Jensen

Michael A. Scaddan ▪ Marcia L. Tate

CORWIN
A SAGE Company

CORWIN
A SAGE Company

FOR INFORMATION:

Corwin

A SAGE Company

2455 Teller Road

Thousand Oaks, California 91320

(800) 233-9936

Fax: (800) 417-2466

www.corwin.com

SAGE Ltd.

1 Oliver's Yard

55 City Road

London EC1Y 1SP

United Kingdom

SAGE India Pvt. Ltd.

B 1/I 1 Mohan Cooperative

Industrial Area

Mathura Road, New Delhi 110 044

India

SAGE Asia-Pacific Pte. Ltd.

33 Pekin Street #02-01

Far East Square

Singapore 048763

Acquisitions Editor: Carol Chambers Collins

Associate Editor: Megan Bedell

Editorial Assistant: Sarah Bartlett

Production Editor: Melanie Birdsall

Typesetter: C&M Digitals (P) Ltd.

Cover Designer: Rose Storey

Permissions Editor: Adele Hutchinson

Printed in the United States of America

Library of Congress Cataloging-in-Publication Data

A catalog record of this book is available from the Library of Congress.

978-1-4522-1734-5

This book is printed on acid-free paper.

11 12 13 14 15 10 9 8 7 6 5 4 3 2 1

Contents

PART III. INSTRUCTIONAL STRATEGIES FOR EVERY BRAIN

Preface

David A. Sousa

Are you curious about all the fuss over "brain-compatible teaching" and learning? Then this introductory book may be just the one for you. For more than two decades, educators, psychologists, and neuroscientists have been exploring whether any of the incredible amount of new information we have learned about the workings of the human brain could be applied to teaching and learning. Little by little, applications became apparent. Now, a new field of inquiry has been established, called *educational neuroscience* (also referred to as *mind, brain, and education*), specifically dedicated to looking for those research findings that have implications for what we do in schools and classrooms. Already, teachers all over the world are revising their instruction, curriculum, and assessment to reflect this new research.

Teachers and school administrators continue to search for ways to include instructional techniques that are supported by brain research into their practice. Corwin has been involved in this area from the beginning. Corwin editors have sought authors who are able to translate research in neuroscience into meaningful and scientifically based instructional strategies. These authors have produced dozens of popular books on brain research. Some of the books focus on new discoveries in brain growth and development. Others are loaded with brain-friendly strategies for all learners, including those learning to read and to calculate, those with special needs, and those who are gifted.

If you are just beginning to explore brain research and its applications to pedagogy, the large number of publications may seem overwhelming. Hence, this book. It is an intriguing smorgasbord, designed to introduce you to samples of the works of eight respected authors, writing in plain language about the applications of neuroscience in different teaching and learning settings. To make this exploration easier, we have divided the book into three parts. Part I focuses on the developing brain and includes chapters on brain structures, on movement, and on the mysteries of the adolescent brain. Part II looks at the brain in school and includes chapters on how the brain learns to read and calculate, on differences between the male and female brain, and on understanding some of the social and academic needs of students with learning difficulties. Part III contains valuable and tested instructional strategies for all students. It includes chapters on reducing stress in the classroom and keeping the students' brain engaged, focused, and energized.

Reading through this book will give you an extensive overview of how much we have learned about teaching and learning in recent years, thanks to the advances in neuroscience. It will also provide you with a substantial collection of strategies and techniques that may help your students become more engaged and successful learners. Our hope, too, is that it will tempt you to read more of these authors' works as part of your own professional development plan. Teachers are brain-changers, and knowing more about how the brain learns can only make them more successful at their job.

Introduction

David A. Sousa

This volume is an overview of the concept of educational neuroscience, featuring excerpts from eleven works by recognized experts. The following is a synopsis of what you will find in each chapter.

PART I. THE DEVELOPING BRAIN

Chapter 1. The Physiology of the Brain

David A. Sousa

Chapter 1 presents an overview of some basic brain structures and their functions in a reader-friendly format and style. It discusses new insights into brain growth and development, such as windows of opportunity, and explains how the brain of today's student has much different expectations of school than the brain of just a decade ago. These modern expectations can pose significant challenges for teachers, and this chapter offers some suggestions on how to deal with them.

Chapter 2. The Child's Brain

Robert Sylwester

Humans are mobile creatures. One daunting challenge facing a toddler's brain is mastering the physiological and cognitive networks that direct movement in all its forms. This intriguing chapter discusses how that process happens and what parents and teachers of young children can do to foster the healthy and robust development of these vital networks.

Chapter 3. The Adolescent's Brain

Sheryl G. Feinstein

Working with adolescents can be challenging, sometimes because of the misconceptions we have about them. This valuable chapter debunks some of the common myths about adolescents and discusses how the various stages of brain development affect teenagers' cognitive, emotional, and physical growth. It offers many practical instructional strategies for getting and maintaining their attention and emphasizes the importance of feedback during the learning process.

PART II. THE BRAIN IN SCHOOL

Chapter 4. The Literate Brain

Pamela Nevills

One of the most difficult tasks we ask the young brain to undertake is to learn to read. Chapter 4 explains how the brain develops pathways to decode reading. It then suggests teaching strategies, such as the importance of connecting reading, writing, and spelling; of identifying word form areas for vocabulary development; and of analytical word analysis. The strategies are research-based and include practical classroom examples.

Chapter 5. The Numerate Brain

David A. Sousa

Children are born with number sense—the ability to approximate and to recognize when objects are added or removed from a group. Number sense develops as the young brain matures, and, eventually, children have to learn to calculate through multiplication, a process that many find difficult. Chapter 5 explains the development of the conceptual structures in the brain that are involved in calculations, and offers instructional strategies for helping children successfully learn multiplication.

Chapter 6. The Male and the Female Brain

Abigail Norfleet James

For decades, parents and educators have debated whether male and female brains learn differently. In Chapter 6, you will read the latest research on gender differences and how these differences may affect learning; certain teaching strategies may be more effective with boys than with girls and vice versa. The chapter also examines how learning disabilities may develop differently in males and females.

Chapter 7. The Special Needs Brain

Eric Jensen

In Chapter 7, we explore the growth and development of the brain's social and academic operating systems. Problems arising in these systems can cause students to have learning difficulties. This chapter offers many suggestions to teachers for helping students build their social skills as well as develop the mindset that can help them overcome academic challenges.

PART III. INSTRUCTIONAL STRATEGIES FOR EVERY BRAIN

Chapter 8. Calming the Brain

Michael A. Scaddan

Stress has a negative impact on learning because it shifts the brain's focus to dealing with the cause of the stress. Chapter 8 suggests proven techniques that teachers can use for lowering stress in students and for raising their motivation to learn.

Chapter 9. Engaging the Brain

Marcia L. Tate

If we expect students to remember what they learn, then the learning must make sense and be relevant. Chapter 9 offers numerous strategies that teachers can use to connect learning to real-world experiences, thus maintaining student interest and increasing retention of learning.

Chapter 10. Focusing the Brain

Marcia L. Tate

Students today are accustomed to constantly interacting with all types of visual media. As a result, visual tools can be powerful instructional devices for capturing students' attention and helping them remember what they learn. Chapter 10 suggests several effective visual organizers that enhance comprehension and the retention of learning.

Chapter 11. Energizing the Brain

Eric Jensen

Recent research has pointed out that movement improves blood flow to the brain, thereby helping it stay focused and engaged during learning. In this chapter, we see how music and other high-energy activities can invigorate students and help them overcome boredom or fatigue.

About the Editor

David A. Sousa, EdD, an international consultant in educational neuroscience, has conducted workshops in hundreds of school districts on brain research and science education at the pre-K to Grade 12 and university levels. He frequently presents at national conventions of educational organizations and to regional and local school districts across the United States, Canada, Europe, Australia, New Zealand, and Asia. Dr. Sousa has a bachelor of science degree in chemistry from Bridgewater (Massachusetts) State University, a master of arts degree in teaching science from Harvard University, and a doctorate from Rutgers University. His teaching experience covers all levels. He has taught high school science and has served as a K–12 director of science, a supervisor of instruction, and a district superintendent in New Jersey schools. He has been an adjunct professor of education at Seton Hall University and a visiting lecturer at Rutgers University. A past president of the National Staff Development Council, Dr. Sousa has edited science books and published numerous articles in leading educational journals on staff development, science education, and brain research. He has received awards from professional associations, school districts, and Bridgewater State University (Distinguished Alumni Award), and several honorary doctorates for his commitment and contributions to research, staff development, and science education. He has been interviewed on the NBC *Today* show and on National Public Radio about his work with schools using brain research.

About the Contributors

Dr. Sheryl Feinstein is an Associate Professor at Augustana College in Sioux Falls, South Dakota, where she teaches in the Education Department. She is the author of a number of books, including *Secrets of the Teenage Brain*, 2nd Ed. (2009), Corwin; *The Praeger Handbook of Learning and the Brain*, 2 vols. (2006), Praeger; *Parenting the Teenage Brain: Understanding a Work in Progress; Teaching the At-Risk Teenage Brain*, and *Inside the Teenage Brain: Understanding a Work in Progress* (2009), Rowman & Littlefield; *101 Insights and Strategies for Parenting Teenagers* (Fall, 2009), Healthy Learning Publishers; and *Tanzanian Women in Their Own Words: Stories of Chronic Illness and Disability* (2009), Lexington Press.

In addition to teaching at Augustana College, Sheryl consults at a correctional facility for adolescent boys and at a separate site for Emotionally/ Behaviorally Disturbed (EBD) adolescents in Minnesota. In 2007–2008, she was awarded a Fulbright Scholarship to Tanzania, where she taught at Tumaini University in Iringa and conducted research involving adolescents. In summer 2006, she was a fellow at Oxford, UK.

Prior to joining the faculty of Augustana College, Sheryl was an administrator for a K–12 school district in Minnesota and taught in the public schools in South Dakota and a private school in Missouri. She can be contacted at sheryl.feinstein@augie.edu.

Abigail Norfleet James taught for many years in single-sex schools and consults on the subject of gendered teaching to school systems, colleges, and universities. Her area of expertise is developmental and educational psychology as applied to the gendered classroom. Prior to obtaining her doctorate from the University of Virginia's Curry School of Education, she taught general science, biology, and psychology in both boys' and girls' schools. Her previous publications include reports of research comparing the educational attitudes of male graduates of coed schools and single-sex schools, research describing the effects of gendered basic skills instruction, and a report of academic achievement of students in single-gender programs. In addition, she has written on differentiated instruction at the elementary school level. She has presented workshops and papers at many educational conferences and works with teachers and parent groups in interpreting the world of gendered education. Her professional affiliations include the American Educational Research Association, the American Psychological Association, the Association for Supervision and Curriculum Development, the Coalition of Schools Educating Boys of Color, the Gender and Education Association, the International Boys' Schools Coalition, and the National Association for Single-Sex Public Education (Advisory Board member).

Eric Jensen is a former teacher with a real love of learning. He has taught at all levels, from elementary through university, and is currently completing his PhD in human development. In 1981, Jensen cofounded SuperCamp (Quantum Learning), the nation's first and largest brain-compatible learning program, now with over fifty thousand graduates. He has since written *Super Teaching, Teaching With the Brain in Mind, Brain-Based Learning, Enriching the Brain,* and 25 other books on learning and the brain. A leader in the brain-based movement, Jensen has made over 65 visits to neuroscience labs and interacts with dozens of neuroscientists annually.

Jensen is currently an active member of the Society for Neuroscience and the New York Academy of Sciences. He was the founder of the Learning Brain EXPO and has trained educators and trainers for 25 years worldwide in this field. He is deeply committed to making a positive, significant, lasting difference in the way we learn. Currently, Jensen does conference speaking, in-school staff development, and in-depth trainings on engagement, enriching students from poverty and student achievement. Go to www.jensen learning.com or e-mail his wife Diane at diane@jlcbrain.com.

Primarily an educator, **Pamela Nevills** held various positions and leadership roles in education. She began as a teacher in grades one through eight and has managed and supervised programs for preschool through high school youth. Her expertise as a staff developer began with a county-level program; later, she managed a curriculum and instruction office. Additional activities include state-level leadership for teacher professional development and student-to-work programs, support for a mathematics research project spanning four states, and two-time participation on a state reading/language arts instructional materials selection panel. Pamela's other positions include supervision for student and intern teachers for the University of California, Riverside, a lecturer for multiple subjects' methodology classes, and she is coauthor with Dr. Patricia Wolfe of the book *Building the Reading Brain.* She is published through the state of California, the *Journal of Staff Development,* and she contributes to organizational newsletters. Of additional and very current interest is her new work emanating from neuroscience with a focus on mathematics.

As an instructor of children and adults, Dr. Nevills studies neurology, mind imaging, and research for education and neurology. By combining information about how the brain functions with learning, she provides insights for teachers to understand memory systems, to engage learners, to maintain attention and concentration, to access the best brain systems to help children become competent readers, and to organize learning for automatic and in depth recall. As a consultant and speaker, she has reached participants both nationally and internationally.

Pamela's website can be found at pamelanevills.com. She can be reached at 1619 Tecalote Drive, Fallbrook, CA 92028; phone (760) 723-8116; e-mail address: panevills@earthlink.net.

Michael A. Scaddan is not only a successful and innovative professional trainer, he has also led a highly successful school down the path of brain-compatible learning. As a principal, he continues to be a practical, hands-on educator, teaching all grade levels of students on a regular basis. This enables him to acquire and develop hundreds of useful and practical classroom tips as well as fine tune the successful schoolwide techniques that he passes on to fellow educators.

Always looking for a better way, he has extensive training in brain-compatible learning. He completed a Masters of Education in accelerated learning and gained certification as a trainer with the Jensen Corporation. Currently Michael offers more than 20 one-to three-day workshops on a wide range of learning topics. He now works as a fulltime learning consultant in the USA, Sweden, Hungary, Singapore, Australia, and New Zealand, and has been an educational consultant to the government of Thailand.

The author can be reached at scaddan.mike@gmail.com.

Robert Sylwester is an emeritus professor of education at the University of Oregon who focuses on the educational implications of new developments in science and technology. He has written 20 books and curricular programs and 200-plus journal articles. His most recent books are *The Adolescent Brain: Reaching for Autonomy* (2007) and *How to Explain a Brain: An Educator's Handbook of Brain Terms and Cognitive Processes* (2005). He received two Distinguished Achievement Awards from The Education Press Association of America for his syntheses of cognitive science research, published in *Educational Leadership*. He has made 1600-plus conference and staff-development presentations on educationally significant developments in brain and stress theory and research. He wrote a monthly column for the Internet journal *Brain Connection,* throughout its 2000 to 2009 existence, and is now a regular contributor to the *Information Age Education Newsletter* (http://i-a-e.org/).

Marcia L. Tate, EdD, is the former executive director of professional development for the DeKalb County School System, Decatur, Georgia. During her 30-year career with the district, she has been a classroom teacher, reading specialist, language arts coordinator, and staff development executive director. She received the Distinguished Staff Development Award for the State of Georgia, and her department was chosen to receive the Exemplary Program Award for the state. More important, Marcia has been married to

Tyrone Tate for more than 30 years and is the proud mother of three wonderful adult children: Jennifer, Jessica, and Christopher; and the doting grandmother of two granddaughters, Christian and Aidan.

Marcia is currently an educational consultant and has taught more than 350,000 parents, teachers, administrators, and business and community leaders throughout the world, including Australia, Egypt, Hungary, Singapore, Thailand, and New Zealand. She is the author of the following five bestsellers: *Worksheets Don't Grow Dendrites: 20 Instructional Strategies That Engage the Brain*; *"Sit & Get" Won't Grow Dendrites: 20 Professional Learning Strategies That Engage the Adult Brain*; *Reading and Language Arts Worksheets Don't Grow Dendrites: 20 Literacy Strategies That Engage the Brain*; *Shouting Won't Grow Dendrites: 20 Techniques for Managing a Brain-Compatible Classroom*; and *Mathematics Worksheets Don't Grow Dendrites: 20 Numeracy Strategies That Engage the Brain*. Her most recent book is *Science Worksheets Don't Grow Dendrites: 20 Instructional Strategies That Engage the Brain*, co-written with Warren Phillips, one of the best science teachers in the country. Participants refer to her workshops as some of the best they have ever experienced, since Marcia uses the 20 brain-compatible strategies outlined in her books to actively engage her audiences.

Marcia received her bachelor's degree in psychology and elementary education from Spelman College in Atlanta, Georgia. She earned her master's degree in remedial reading from the University of Michigan, her specialist degree in educational leadership from Georgia State University, and her doctorate in educational leadership from Clark Atlanta University. Spelman College awarded her the Apple Award for excellence in the field of education.

Marcia and her husband own the consulting firm Developing Minds Inc. and can be contacted by calling (770) 918-5039 or by e-mail: marciata@ bellsouth.net. Visit her website at www.developingmindsinc.com.

Part I

The Developing Brain

Chapter 1

The Physiology of the Brain

David A. Sousa

With our new knowledge of the brain, we are just dimly beginning to realize that we can now understand humans, including ourselves, as never before, and that this is the greatest advance of the century, and quite possibly the most significant in all human history.

—Leslie A. Hart
Human Brain and Human Learning

Chapter Highlights: This chapter introduces some of the basic structures of the human brain and their functions. It explores the growth of the young brain and some of the environmental factors that influence its development into adolescence. Whether the brain of today's student is compatible with today's schools and the impact of technology are also discussed.

The adult human brain is a wet, fragile mass that weighs a little more than three pounds. It is about the size of a small grapefruit, is shaped like a walnut, and can fit in the palm of your hand. Cradled in the skull and surrounded by protective membranes, it is poised at the top of the spinal column. The brain works ceaselessly, even when we are asleep. Although it represents only about 2 percent of our body weight, it consumes nearly 20 percent of our calories! The more we think, the more calories we burn. Perhaps this can be a new diet fad, and we could modify Descartes' famous quotation from "I think, therefore I am" to "I think, therefore I'm thin"!

Through the centuries, surveyors of the brain have examined every cerebral feature, sprinkling the landscape with Latin and Greek names to describe what they saw. They analyzed structures and functions and sought concepts to explain their observations. One early concept divided the brain by location—forebrain, midbrain, and hindbrain. Another, proposed by Paul MacLean (1990) in the 1960s, described the triune brain according to three stages of evolution: reptilian (brain stem), paleo-mammalian (limbic area), and mammalian (frontal lobes).

For our purposes, we will take a look at major parts of the outside of the brain (Figure 1.1). We will then look at the inside of the brain and divide it into three parts on the basis of their general functions: the brain stem, limbic system, and cerebrum (Figure 1.2). We will also examine the structure of the brain's nerve cells, called *neurons*.

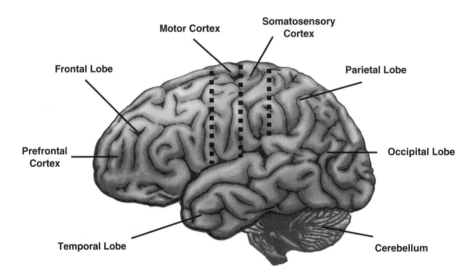

Figure 1.1   The major exterior regions of the brain.

SOME EXTERIOR PARTS OF THE BRAIN

Lobes of the Brain

Although the minor wrinkles are unique in each brain, several major wrinkles and folds are common to all brains. These folds form a set of four lobes in each hemisphere. Each lobe tends to specialize for certain functions.

Frontal Lobes. At the front of the brain are the *frontal lobes*, and the part lying just behind the forehead is called the *prefrontal cortex*. Often called the executive control center, these lobes deal with planning and thinking. They comprise the rational and executive control center of the brain, monitoring higher-order thinking, directing problem solving, and regulating the excesses of the emotional system. The frontal lobe also contains our self-will area—what some might call our personality. Trauma to the frontal lobe can cause dramatic—and sometimes permanent—behavior and personality changes. Because most of the working memory is located here, it is the area where focus occurs (Geday & Gjedde, 2009; E. E. Smith & Jonides, 1999). The frontal lobe matures slowly. MRI studies of postadolescents reveal that the frontal lobe continues to mature into early adulthood. Thus, the capability of the frontal lobe to control the excesses of the emotional system is not fully operational during adolescence (Dosenbach et al., 2010; Goldberg, 2001). This is one important reason why adolescents are more likely than adults to submit to their emotions and resort to high-risk behavior.

> *Because the rational system matures slowly in adolescents, they are more likely to submit to their emotions.*

Temporal Lobes. Above the ears rest the *temporal lobes*, which deal with sound, music, face and object recognition, and some parts of long-term memory. They also house the speech centers, although this is usually on the left side only.

Occipital Lobes. At the back are the paired *occipital lobes*, which are used almost exclusively for visual processing.

Parietal Lobes. Near the top are the *parietal lobes*, which deal mainly with spatial orientation, calculation, and certain types of recognition.

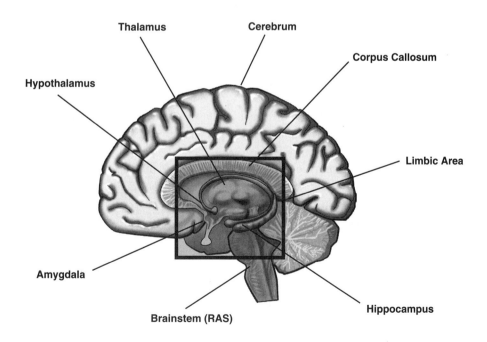

Figure 1.2 A cross section of the human brain.

Motor Cortex and Somatosensory Cortex

Between the parietal and frontal lobes are two bands across the top of the brain from ear to ear. The band closer to the front is the *motor cortex*. This strip controls body movement and, as we will learn later, works with the cerebellum to coordinate the learning of motor skills. Just behind the motor cortex, at the beginning of the parietal lobe, is the *somatosensory cortex,* which processes touch signals received from various parts of the body.

SOME INTERIOR PARTS OF THE BRAIN

Brain Stem

The brain stem is the oldest and deepest area of the brain. It is often referred to as the reptilian brain because it resembles the entire brain of a reptile. Of the 12 body nerves that go to the brain, 11 end in the brain stem (the olfactory nerve—for smell—goes directly to the limbic system, an evolutionary artifact). Here is where vital body functions, such as heartbeat, respiration, body temperature, and digestion, are monitored and controlled. The brain stem also houses the reticular activating system (RAS), responsible for the brain's alertness and about which more will be explained in the next chapter.

The Limbic System

Nestled above the brain stem and below the cerebrum lies a collection of structures commonly referred to as the limbic system and sometimes called the old mammalian brain. Many researchers now caution that viewing the limbic system as a separate functional entity is outdated because all of its components interact with many other areas of the brain.

Most of the structures in the limbic system are duplicated in each hemisphere of the brain. These structures carry out a number of different functions including the generation of emotions and processing emotional memories. Its placement between the cerebrum and the brain stem permits the interplay of emotion and reason.

Four parts of the limbic system are important to learning and memory. They include the following:

The Thalamus. All incoming sensory information (except smell) goes first to the thalamus (Greek for "inner chamber"). From here it is directed to other parts of the brain for additional processing. The cerebrum and the cerebellum also send signals to the thalamus, thus involving it in many cognitive activities, including memory.

The Hypothalamus. Nestled just below the thalamus is the hypothalamus. While the thalamus monitors information coming in from the outside, the hypothalamus monitors the internal systems to maintain the normal state of the body (called *homeostasis*). By controlling the release of a variety of hormones, it moderates numerous body functions, including sleep, body temperature, food intake, and liquid intake. If body systems slip out of balance, it is difficult for the individual to concentrate on cognitive processing of curriculum material.

The Hippocampus. Located near the base of the limbic area is the hippocampus (the Greek word for "sea horse," because of its shape). It plays a major role in consolidating learning and in converting information from working memory via electrical signals to the long-term storage regions, a process that may take days to months. It constantly checks information relayed to working memory and compares it to stored experiences. This process is essential for the creation of meaning.

Its role was first revealed by patients whose hippocampus was damaged or removed because of disease. These patients could remember everything that happened before the operation, but not afterward. If they were introduced to you today, you would be a stranger to them tomorrow. Because they can remember information for only a few minutes, they can read the same article repeatedly and believe on each occasion that it is the first time they have read it. Brain scans have confirmed the role of the hippocampus in permanent memory storage. Alzheimer's disease progressively destroys neurons in the hippocampus, resulting in memory loss.

Recent studies of brain-damaged patients have revealed that although the hippocampus plays an important role in the recall of facts, objects, and places, it does not seem to play much of a role in the recall of long-term personal memories (Lieberman, 2005). One surprising revelation in recent years is that the hippocampus has the capability to produce new neurons—a process called *neurogenesis*—into adulthood (Balu & Lucki, 2009). Furthermore, there is research evidence that this form of neurogenesis has a significant impact on learning and memory (Deng, Aimone, & Gage, 2010; Neves, Cooke, & Bliss, 2008). Studies also reveal that neurogenesis can be strengthened by diet (Kitamura, Mishina, & Sugiyama, 2006) and exercise (Pereira et al., 2007) and weakened by prolonged sleep loss (Meerlo, Mistlberger, Jacobs, Heller, & McGinty, 2009).

> *Neurogenesis—the growth of new neurons—can be strengthened by diet and exercise and weakened by prolonged sleep loss.*

The Amygdala. Attached to the end of the hippocampus is the amygdala (Greek for "almond"). This structure plays an important role in emotions, especially fear. It regulates the individual's interactions with the environment that can affect survival, such as whether to attack, escape, mate, or eat.

Because of its proximity to the hippocampus and its activity on PET scans, researchers believe that the amygdala encodes an emotional message, if one is present, whenever a memory is tagged for long-term storage. It is not known at this time whether the emotional memories themselves are actually stored in the amygdala. One possibility is that the emotional component of a memory is stored in the amygdala while other cognitive components (names, dates, etc.) are stored elsewhere (Squire & Kandel, 1999). The emotional component is recalled whenever the memory is recalled. This explains why people recalling a strong emotional memory will often experience those emotions again. The interactions between the amygdala and the hippocampus ensure that we remember for a long time those events that are important and emotional.

Teachers, of course, hope that their students will permanently remember what was taught. Therefore, it is intriguing to realize that the two structures in the brain mainly responsible for long-term remembering are located in the *emotional* area of the brain. Understanding the connection between emotions and cognitive learning and memory will be discussed in later chapters.

Test Question No. 1: The structures responsible for deciding what gets stored in long-term memory are located in the brain's rational system.

Answer: False. These structures are located in the emotional (limbic) system.

Cerebrum

A soft, jellylike mass, the cerebrum is the largest area, representing nearly 80 percent of the brain by weight. Its surface is pale gray, wrinkled, and marked by deep furrows called *fissures* and shallow ones called *sulci* (singular, *sulcus*). Raised folds are called *gyri* (singular, *gyrus*). One large sulcus runs from front to back and divides the cerebrum into two halves, called the *cerebral hemispheres*. For some still unexplained reason, the nerves from the left side of the body cross over to the right hemisphere, and those from the right side of the body cross to the left hemisphere. The two hemispheres are connected by a thick cable of more than 200 million nerve fibers called the *corpus callosum* (Latin for "large body"). The hemispheres use this bridge to communicate with each other and coordinate activities.

The hemispheres are covered by a thin but tough laminated *cortex* (meaning "tree bark"), rich in cells, that is about one tenth of an inch thick and, because of its folds, has a surface area of about two square feet. That is about the size of a large dinner napkin. The cortex is composed of six layers of cells meshed in about 10,000 miles of connecting fibers per cubic inch! Here is where most of the action takes place. Thinking, memory, speech, and muscular movement are controlled by areas in the cerebrum. The cortex is often referred to as the brain's gray matter.

The neurons in the thin cortex form columns whose branches extend through the cortical layer into a dense web below known as the white matter. Here, neurons connect with each other to form vast arrays of neural networks that carry out specific functions.

Cerebellum

The cerebellum (Latin for "little brain") is a two-hemisphere structure located just below the rear part of the cerebrum, right behind the brain stem. Representing about 11 percent of the brain's weight, it is a deeply folded and highly organized structure containing more neurons than all of the rest of the brain put together. The surface area of the entire cerebellum is about the same as that of one of the cerebral hemispheres.

This area coordinates movement. Because the cerebellum monitors impulses from nerve endings in the muscles, it is important in the performance and timing of complex motor tasks. It modifies and coordinates commands to swing a golf club, smooth a dancer's footsteps, and allow a hand to bring a cup to the lips without spilling its contents. The cerebellum may also store the memory of automated movements, such as touch-typing and tying a shoelace. Through such automation, performance can be improved as the sequences of movements can be made with greater speed, greater accuracy, and less effort. The cerebellum also is known to be involved in the mental rehearsal of motor tasks, which also can improve performance and make it more skilled. A person whose cerebellum is damaged slows down and simplifies movement, and would have difficulty with finely tuned motion, such as catching a ball or completing a handshake.

Recent studies indicate that the role of the cerebellum has been underestimated. Researchers now believe that it also acts as a support structure in cognitive processing by coordinating and fine-tuning our thoughts, emotions, senses (especially touch), and memories. Because the cerebellum is connected also to regions of the brain that perform mental and sensory tasks, it can perform these skills automatically, without conscious attention to detail. This allows the conscious part of the brain the freedom to attend to other mental activities, thus enlarging its cognitive scope. Such enlargement of human capabilities is attributable in no small part to the cerebellum and its contribution to the automation of numerous mental activities.

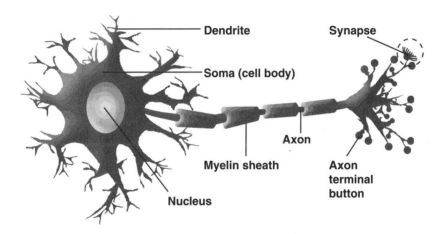

Figure 1.3 Neurons transmit signals along an axon and across the synapse (in dashed circle) to the dendrites of a neighboring cell. The myelin sheath protects the axon and increases the speed of transmission.

Brain Cells

The brain is composed of a trillion cells of at least two known types, nerve cells and glial cells. The nerve cells are called *neurons* and represent about a tenth of the total—roughly 100 billion. Most of the cells are *glial* (Greek for "glue") cells that hold the neurons together and act as filters to keep harmful substances out of the neurons. Very recent studies indicate that some star-shaped glial cells, called *astrocytes*, have a role in regulating the rate of neuron signaling. By attaching themselves to blood vessels, astrocytes also serve to form the blood-brain barrier, which plays an important role in protecting brain cells from blood-borne substances that could disrupt cellular activity.

The neurons are the functioning core for the brain and the entire nervous system. Neurons come in different sizes, but the body of each brain neuron is about one hundredth of the size of the period at the end of this sentence. These cells were first discovered in the late 1800s by Santiago Ramón y Cajal (1989), a Spanish neuroscientist. Unlike other cells, the neuron (see Figure 1.3) has tens of thousands of branches emerging from its core, called *dendrites* (from the Greek word for "tree"). The dendrites receive electrical impulses from other neurons and transmit them along a long fiber, called the *axon* (Greek for "axis"). There is normally only one axon per neuron. A layer called the *myelin sheath* surrounds each axon. The sheath insulates the axon from the other cells and increases the speed of impulse transmission. This impulse travels along the neurons through an electrochemical process and can move through the entire length of a six-foot adult in two tenths of a second. A neuron can transmit between 250 and 2,500 impulses per second.

Neurons have no direct contact with each other. Between each dendrite and axon is a small gap of about a millionth of an inch called a *synapse* (from the Greek, meaning "to join together"). A typical neuron collects signals from others through the dendrites, which are covered at the synapse with thousands of tiny bumps, called *spines*. The neuron sends out spikes of electrical activity (impulses) through the axon to the synapse where the activity releases chemicals stored in sacs (called *synaptic vesicles*) at the end of the axon (Figure 1.4). These chemicals, called *neurotransmitters*, either excite or inhibit the neighboring neuron. More than 50 different neurotransmitters have been discovered so far. Some of the common neurotransmitters are acetylcholine, epinephrine, serotonin, and dopamine. Learning occurs by changing the synapses so that the influence of one neuron on another also changes.

A direct connection seems to exist between the physical world of the brain and the work of the brain's owner. Recent studies of neurons in people of different occupations (e.g., professional musicians) show that the more complex the skills demanded of the occupation, the greater the number of dendrites that were found on the neurons. This increase in dendrites allows for more connections between neurons resulting in more sites in which to store learnings.

There are about 100 billion neurons in the adult human brain—about 16 times as many neurons as people on this planet and about the number of stars in the Milky Way. Each neuron can have up to 10,000 dendrite branches. This means that it is possible to have up to one quadrillion (that's a 1 followed by 15 zeros) synaptic connections in one brain. This inconceivably large number allows the brain to process the data coming continuously from the senses; to store decades of memories, faces, and places; to learn languages; and to combine information in a way that no other individual on this planet has ever thought of before. This is a remarkable achievement for just three pounds of soft tissue!

> *Believe it or not, the number of potential synaptic connections in just one human brain is about 1,000,000,000,000,000.*

Conventional wisdom has been that neurons were the only body cells that never regenerate. However, we noted earlier that researchers have discovered that the adult human brain does generate neurons in at least one site—the hippocampus. This discovery raises the question of whether neurons regenerate in other parts of the brain and, if so, if it might be possible to stimulate them to repair and heal damaged brains, especially for the growing number of people with Alzheimer's disease. Research into Alzheimer's disease is exploring ways to stop the deadly mechanisms that trigger the destruction of neurons.

Mirror Neurons

Scientists using fMRI technology discovered clusters of neurons in the premotor cortex (the area in front of the motor cortex that plans movements) firing just before a person carried out a planned movement. Curiously, these neurons also fired when a person saw someone else perform the same movement. For example, the firing pattern of these neurons that preceded the subject grasping a cup of coffee was identical to the pattern when the subject saw someone else do that. Thus, similar brain areas process both the production and the perception of movement. Neuroscientists believe these *mirror neurons* may help an individual to decode the intentions and predict the behavior of others. They allow us to re-create the experience of others within ourselves, and to understand others' emotions and empathize. Seeing the look of disgust or joy on other people's faces causes mirror neurons to trigger similar emotions in us. We start to feel their actions and sensations as though we were doing them.

Mirror neurons probably explain the mimicry we see in young children when they imitate our smile and many of our other movements. We have all experienced this phenomenon when we attempted to stifle a yawn after seeing someone else yawning. Neuroscientists believe that mirror neurons may explain a lot about mental behaviors that have remained a mystery. For instance, there is experimental evidence that children with autism have a deficit in their mirror-neuron system. That would explain why they have difficulty inferring the intentions and mental state of others (Oberman et al., 2005). Researchers also suspect that mirror neurons play a role in our ability to develop articulate speech (Arbib, 2005).

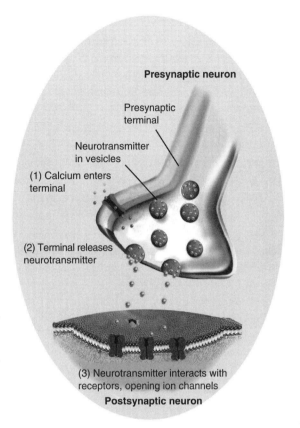

Figure 1.4 The neural impulse is carried across the synapse by chemicals called neurotransmitters that lie within the synaptic vesicles.

Brain Fuel

Brain cells consume oxygen and glucose (a form of sugar) for fuel. The more challenging the brain's task, the more fuel it consumes. Therefore, it is important to have adequate amounts of these substances in the brain for optimum functioning. Low amounts of oxygen and glucose in the blood can produce lethargy and sleepiness. Eating a moderate portion of food containing glucose (fruits are an excellent source) can boost the performance and accuracy of working

> **Many students (and their teachers) do not eat a breakfast with sufficient glucose or drink enough water during the day for healthy brain function.**

memory, attention, and motor function (Korol & Gold, 1998; Scholey, Moss, Neave, & Wesnes, 1999), as well as improve long-term recognition memory (Sünram-Lea, Dewhurst, & Foster, 2008).

Water, also essential for healthy brain activity, is required to move neuron signals through the brain. Low concentrations of water diminish the rate and efficiency of these signals. Moreover, water keeps the lungs sufficiently moist to allow for the efficient transfer of oxygen into the bloodstream.

Many students (and their teachers, too) do not eat a breakfast that contains sufficient glucose, nor do they drink enough water during the day to maintain healthy brain function. Schools should have breakfast programs and educate students on the need to have sufficient blood levels of glucose during the day. Schools should also provide frequent opportunities for students and staff to drink plenty of water. The current recommended amount is an eight-ounce glass of water a day for every 25 pounds of body weight.

NEURON DEVELOPMENT IN CHILDREN

Neuron development starts in the embryo about four weeks after conception and proceeds at an astonishing rate. In the first four months of gestation, about 200 billion neurons are formed, but about half will die off during the fifth month because they fail to connect with any areas of the growing embryo. This purposeful destruction of neurons (called *apoptosis*) is genetically programmed to ensure that only those neurons that have made connections are preserved, and to prevent the brain from being overcrowded with unconnected cells. The characteristic folds in the cerebrum begin to develop around the sixth month of gestation, creating the sulci and gyri that give the brain its wrinkled look. Any drugs or alcohol that the mother takes during this time can interfere with the growing brain cells, increasing the risk of fetal addiction and mental defects.

The neurons of a newborn are immature; many of their axons lack the protective myelin layer, and there are few connections between them. Thus, most regions of the cerebral cortex are quiet. Understandably, the most active areas are the brain stem (body functions) and the cerebellum (movement).

The neurons in a child's brain make many more connections than those in adults. A newborn's brain makes connections at an incredible pace as the child absorbs its environment. Information is entering the brain through "windows" that emerge and taper off at various times. The richer the environment, the greater the number of interconnections that are made. Consequently, learning can take place faster and with greater meaning.

As the child approaches puberty, the pace slackens, and two other processes begin: Connections the brain finds useful become permanent; those not useful are eliminated (apoptosis) as the brain selectively strengthens and prunes connections based on experience. This process continues throughout our lives, but it appears to be most intense between the ages of 3 and 12 years. Thus, at an early age, experiences are already shaping the brain and designing the unique neural architecture that will influence how it handles future experiences in school, work, and other places.

Windows of Opportunity

Windows of opportunity represent important periods in which the young brain responds to certain types of input from its environment to create or consolidate neural networks. Some windows relating to physical development are critical, and are called *critical periods* by pediatric researchers. For example, if even a perfect brain doesn't receive visual stimuli by the age of 2, the child will be forever blind, and if it doesn't hear words by the age of 12, the person will most likely never learn a language. When these critical windows taper off, the brain cells assigned to those tasks may be pruned or recruited for other tasks (M. Diamond & Hopson, 1998).

The windows relating to cognitive and skill development are far more plastic, but still significant. It is important to remember that learning can occur in each of the areas for the rest of our lives, even after a window tapers off. However, the skill level probably will not be as high. This ability of the brain to continually change during our lifetime in subtle ways as a result of experience is referred to as *plasticity*.

An intriguing question is why the windows taper off so early in life, especially since the average life span is now more than 75 years of age. One possible explanation is that these developmental spurts are genetically determined and were set in place many thousands of years ago when our life span was closer to 20 years. Figure 1.5 shows just a few of the windows that we will examine to understand their importance.

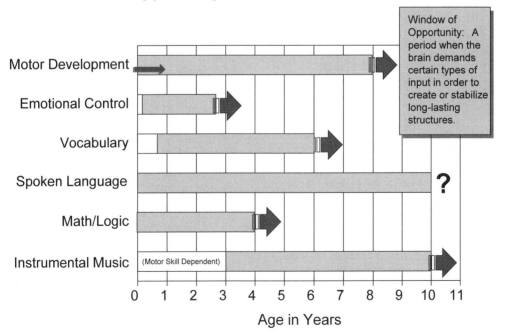

Figure 1.5 The chart shows some of the sensitive periods for learning during childhood, according to current research. Future studies may modify the ranges shown in the chart. It is important to remember that learning occurs throughout our entire life.

A word of caution is necessary here. The notion of windows of opportunity should not cause parents to worry that they may have missed providing critical experiences to their children in their early years. Rather, parents and educators should remember that the brain's plasticity and resilience allow it to learn almost anything at any time. In general, learning earlier is better, but learning later is not a catastrophe.

Motor Development

This window opens during fetal development. Those who have borne children remember all too well the movement of the fetus during the third trimester as motor connections and systems are consolidating. The child's ability to learn motor skills appears to be most pronounced in the first eight years. Such seemingly simple tasks as crawling and walking require complicated associations of neural networks, including integrating information from the balance sensors in the inner ear and output signals to the leg and arm muscles. Of course, a person can learn motor skills after the window tapers off. However, what is learned while it is open can be learned masterfully. For example, most concert virtuosos, Olympic medalists, and professional players of individual sports (e.g., tennis and golf) began practicing their skills by the age of 8.

> **What is learned while a window of opportunity is opened can be learned masterfully.**

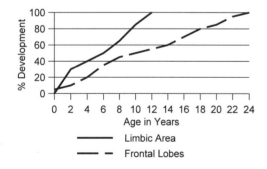

Development of the Brain's Limbic Area and Frontal Lobes

% Development vs. Age in Years

—— Limbic Area

– – Frontal Lobes

Figure 1.6 Based on research studies, this chart suggests the possible degree of development of the brain's limbic area and frontal lobes. The 10- to 12-year lag in the full development of the frontal lobes (the brain's rational system) explains why so many adolescents and young adults get involved in risky situations.

Emotional Control

The window for developing emotional control seems to be from 2 to 30 months. During that time, the limbic (emotional) system and the frontal lobe's rational system are evaluating each other's ability to get their owner what it wants. It is hardly a fair match. Studies of human brain growth suggest that the emotional (and older) system develops faster than the frontal lobes (Figure 1.6) (Beatty, 2001; Gazzaniga, Ivry, & Mangun, 2002; Goldberg, 2001; Luciana, Conklin, Hooper, & Yarger, 2005; Paus, 2005; Restak, 2001; Steinberg, 2005). Consequently, the emotional system is more likely to win the tug-of-war for control. If tantrums almost always get the child satisfaction when the window is open, then that is the method the child will likely use when the window tapers off. This constant emotional-rational battle is one of the major contributors to the "terrible twos." Certainly, one can learn to control emotions after that age. But what the child learned during that open-window period will be difficult to change, and it will strongly influence what is learned after the window tapers off.

> **The struggle between the emotional and rational systems is a major contributor to the "terrible twos."**

In an astonishing example of how nurturing can influence nature, there is considerable evidence confirming that how parents respond to their children emotionally during this time frame can encourage or stifle genetic tendencies. Biology is not destiny, so gene expression is not necessarily inevitable. To produce their effects, genes must be turned on. The cells on the tip of your nose contain the same genetic code as those in your stomach lining. But the gene that codes for producing stomach acid is activated in your stomach, yet idled on your nose. For example, shyness is a trait that seems to be partially hereditary. If parents are overprotective of their bashful young daughter, the toddler is likely to remain shy. On the other hand, if they encourage her to interact with other toddlers, she may overcome it. Thus, genetic tendencies toward intelligence, sociability, or schizophrenia and aggression can be ignited, moderated, or stifled by parental response and other environmental influences (Reiss, Neiderheiser, Hetherington, & Plomin, 2000).

Vocabulary

Because the human brain is genetically predisposed for language, babies start uttering sounds and babble nonsense phrases as early as the age of 2 months. By the age of 8 months, infants begin to try out simple words like *mama* and *dada*. The language areas of the brain become really active at 18 to 20 months. A toddler can learn 10 or more words per day, yielding a vocabulary of about 900 words at age 3 years, increasing to 2,500 to 3,000 words by the age of 5.

Here's testimony to the power of talk: Researchers have shown that babies whose parents, especially fathers, talked to them more had significantly larger vocabularies (Pancsofar & Vernon-Feagans, 2006). Knowing a word is not the same as understanding its meaning. So it is crucial for parents to encourage their children to use new words in a context that demonstrates they know what the words mean. Children who know the meaning of most of the words in their large vocabulary will start school with a greater likelihood that learning to read will be easier and quicker.

Language Acquisition

The newborn's brain is not the *tabula rasa* (blank slate) we once thought. Certain areas are specialized for specific stimuli, including spoken language. The window for acquiring spoken language opens soon after birth and tapers off first around the age of 5 years and again around the age of 10 to 12 years. Beyond that age, learning any language becomes more difficult. The genetic impulse to learn language is so strong that children found in feral environments often make up their own language. There is also evidence that the human ability to acquire grammar may have a specific window of opportunity in the early years (M. Diamond & Hopson, 1998; Pulvermüller, 2010). Knowing this, it seems illogical that many schools still wait to *start* new language instruction in middle school or high school rather than in the primary grades. Chapter 5 deals in greater detail with how the brain acquires spoken language.

Mathematics and Logic

How and when the young brain understands numbers is uncertain, but there is mounting evidence that infants have a rudimentary number sense that is wired into certain brain sites at birth (Butterworth, 1999; Dehaene, 2010; Devlin, 2000). The purpose of these sites is to categorize the world in terms of the "number of things" in a collection; that is, they can tell the difference between two of something and three of something. We drive along a road and see horses in a field. While we are noticing that they are brown and black, we cannot help but see that there are four of them, even though we did not count them individually. Researchers have also found that toddlers as young as 2 years recognize the relationships between numbers as large as 4 and 5, even though they are not able to verbally label them. This research shows that fully functioning language ability is not needed to support numerical thinking (Brannon & van der Walle, 2001), but is necessary to do numerical calculations (Dehaene, 2010).

Instrumental Music

All cultures create music, so we can assume that it is an important part of being human. Babies respond to music as early as 2 to 3 months of age. A window for creating music may be open at birth, but obviously neither the baby's vocal chords nor motor skills are adequate to sing or to play an instrument. Around the age of 3 years, most toddlers have sufficient manual dexterity to play a piano (Mozart was playing the harpsichord and composing at age 4). Several studies have shown that children ages 3 to 4 years who received piano lessons scored significantly higher in spatial-temporal tasks than a group who did not get the instrumental music training. Further, the increase was long term. Brain imaging reveals that creating instrumental music excites the same regions of the left frontal lobe responsible for mathematics and logic. See Chapter 6 for more on the effects of music on the brain and learning.

> *School districts should communicate with the parents of newborns and offer their services and resources to help parents succeed as the first teachers of their children.*

Research on how the young brain develops suggests that an enriched home and preschool environment during the early years can help children build neural connections and make full use of their mental abilities. Because of the importance of early years, I believe school districts should communicate with the parents of newborns and offer their services and resources to help parents succeed as the first teachers of their children. Such programs are already in place on a statewide basis in Michigan, Missouri, and Kentucky, and similar programs sponsored by local school districts are springing up elsewhere. But we need to work faster toward achieving this important goal.

THE BRAIN AS A NOVELTY SEEKER

Part of our success as a species can be attributed to the brain's persistent interest in novelty, that is, changes occurring in the environment. The brain is constantly scanning its environment for stimuli. When an unexpected stimulus arises—such as a loud noise from an empty room—a rush of adrenaline closes down all unnecessary activity and focuses the brain's attention so it can spring into action. Conversely, an environment that contains mainly predictable or repeated stimuli (like some classrooms?) lowers the brain's interest in the outside world and tempts it to turn within for novel sensations.

Environmental Factors That Enhance Novelty

Craig is a good friend of mine and a high school mathematics teacher with more than 20 years' experience. He often remarks about how different today's students are from those of just a few years ago. They arrive with all their electronic gadgets and their attention darting among many tasks—usually not involving mathematics. As a conscientious teacher, Craig has incorporated more technology in his lessons, mainly because that holds his students' attention. In the past, Craig smiled skeptically whenever I talked to him about the rapidly increasing research findings about the brain and their possible applications to teaching and learning. Not anymore! He now realizes that because the brain of today's student is developing in a rapidly changing environment, he must adjust his teaching.

We often hear teachers remark that students are more different today in the way they learn than ever before. They seem to have shorter attention spans and bore easily. Why is that? Is there something happening in the environment of learners that alters the way they approach the learning process?

The Environment of the Past

The home environment for many children several decades ago was quite different from that of today. For example,

- The home was quieter—some might say boring compared to today.
- Parents and children did a lot of talking and reading.

- The family unit was more stable, family members ate together, and the dinner hour was an opportunity for parents to discuss their children's activities as well as reaffirm their love and support.
- If the home had a television, it was in a common area and controlled by adults. What children watched could be carefully monitored.
- School was an interesting place because it had television, films, field trips, and guest speakers. Because there were few other distractions, school was an important influence in a child's life and the primary source of information.
- The neighborhood was also an important part of growing up. Children played together, developing their motor skills as well as learning the social skills needed to develop relationships and interact successfully with other children in the neighborhood.

The Environment of Today

In recent years, children have been growing up in a very different environment.

- Family units are not as stable as they once were. Single-parent families are more common, and in 2007 represented 26.3 percent of all households in the United States with children under the age of 21 (Grall, 2009). That totals to more than 5.7 million children. Their dietary habits are changing as home cooking is becoming a lost art. As a result, children have fewer opportunities to have that important dinnertime talk with the adults who care for them.
- Many 10- to 18-year-olds can now watch television and play with other technology in their own bedrooms, leading to sleep deprivation. Furthermore, with no adult present, what kind of moral compass is evolving in the impressionable preadolescent mind as a result of watching programs containing violence and sex on television and the Internet?
- They get information from many different sources beside school, some of it inaccurate or false.
- They spend much more time indoors with their technology, thereby missing outdoor opportunities to develop gross motor skills and socialization skills necessary to communicate and act personally and civilly with others. One unintended consequence of spending so much time indoors is the rapid rise in the number of overweight children and adolescents, now more than 17 percent of 6- to 19-year-olds (Centers for Disease Control and Prevention, 2010).
- Young brains have responded to the technology by changing their functioning and organization to accommodate the large amount of stimulation occurring in the environment. By acclimating themselves to these changes, brains respond more than ever to the unique and different—what is called novelty. There is a dark side to this increased novelty-seeking behavior. Some adolescents who perceive little novelty in their environment may turn to mind-altering drugs, such as ecstasy and amphetamines, for stimulation. This drug dependence can further enhance the brain's demand for novelty to the point that it becomes unbalanced and resorts to extremely risky behavior.

- Their diet contains increasing amounts of substances that can affect brain and body functions. Caffeine is a strong brain stimulant, considered safe for most adults in small quantities. But caffeine is found in many of the foods and drinks that teens consume daily. Too much caffeine causes insomnia, anxiety, and nausea. Some teens can also develop allergies to aspartame (an artificial sugar found in children's vitamins and many "lite" foods) and other food additives. Possible symptoms of these allergic reactions include hyperactivity, difficulty concentrating, and headaches (Bateman et al., 2004; Millichap & Yee, 2003).

When we add to this mix the changes in family lifestyles and the temptations of alcohol and drugs, we can realize how very different the environment of today's child is from that of just 15 years ago.

How Is Technology Affecting the Student's Brain?

Students today are surrounded by media: cell phones, smartphones, multiple televisions, MP3 players, movies, computers, video games, iPads, e-mail, and the Internet. Eight- to 18-year-olds spend an average of seven hours per day with digital media (Rideout, Foehr, & Roberts, 2010). The multimedia environment divides their attention. Even newscasts are different. In the past, only the reporter's face was on the screen. Now, the TV screen I am looking at is loaded with information. Three people are reporting in from different corners of the world. Additional nonrelated news is scrolling across the bottom, and the stock market averages are changing in

> *The brain cannot multitask. It can focus on only one task at a time. Alternating between tasks always incurs a loss.*

the lower right-hand corner just below the local time and temperature. For me, these tidbits are distracting and are forcing me to split my attention into several components. I find myself missing a reporter's comment because a scrolling item caught my attention. Yet, children have become accustomed to these information-rich and rapidly changing messages. They can shift their attention quickly among several things, but their brains can still focus on only one thing at a time.

The Myth of Multitasking. Sure, we can walk and chew gum at the same time because they are separate physical tasks requiring no measurable cognitive input. However, the brain cannot carry out two cognitive processes simultaneously. Our genetic predisposition for survival directs the brain to focus on just one item at a time to determine whether it poses a threat. If we were able to focus on several items at once, it would dilute our attention and seriously reduce our ability to make the threat determination quickly and accurately.

What we refer to as multitasking is actually task switching. It occurs as sequential tasking (attention moves from Item A to Item B to Item C, etc.) or alternate tasking (attention moves between Items A and B). Whenever the brain shifts from focusing on Item A to focusing on Item B

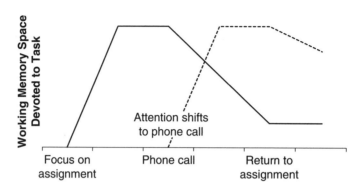

Figure 1.7   When an assignment is interrupted by a phone call, memory resources dedicated to the assignment (solid line) decline, and resources dealing with information from the phone call (dotted line) increase.

and back again to Item A, there is a cognitive loss involved. Figure 1.7 illustrates the process that will unfold in the following example. The solid graph line represents the amount of working memory used to process a homework task, and the dotted graph line represents the amount used to process an incoming phone call. Let us say Jeremy is a high school student who is working on a history assignment and has just spent 10 minutes focusing on understanding the major causes of World War II. The thinking part of his brain is working hard, and a significant amount of working memory is processing this information.

Suddenly, the cell phone rings. It is Jeremy's girlfriend, Donna. As he answers the phone, his brain must disengage from processing history information to recalling the steps to answering and attending to a phone call. Jeremy spends the next six minutes chatting with Donna. During that time, much of the World War II information that Jeremy's working memory was processing begins to fade as it is replaced by information from the phone call. (Working memory has a limited capacity.) When Jeremy returns to the assignment, it is almost like starting all over again. The memory of having worked on the assignment may cause the student to believe that all the information is still in working memory, but much of it is gone. He may even mumble, "OK, where was I?" The task of switching tasks incurs a price (Monk, Trafton, & Boehm-Davis, 2008). Some studies indicate that a person who is interrupted during a task may take up to 50 percent longer to finish the task and make up to 50 percent more errors (Medina, 2008).

Task Switching and Complex Texts. Living in a world where task switching is the norm may be affecting a student's ability to read and concentrate on complex texts. In a 2006 report, the assessment and research firm ACT examined the readiness of high school graduates to tackle the reading required of college texts and technical manuals. The study found that there was no significant difference between the scores of students who were college bound and those who were not in the areas of reading for the main idea, the meaning of words, supporting evidence, generalizations, and conclusions. Another finding was that the one reading measure that clearly differentiated between college-bound and non-college-bound students was the ability to comprehend complex texts. These texts usually contain high-level vocabulary and elaborate grammatical structure, as well as literal and inferred meanings. ACT noted that a little more than half of the high school graduates were able to meet the demands of first-year college-level reading, based on a national readiness indicator.

Is it possible that high school students have become so adapted to task switching that they have not developed the cognitive discipline necessary to read complex tests? Bauerlein (2011) suggests that successfully reading complex texts demands the following three skills that constantly wired students may not be developing:

1. A willingness to probe an author's writings for literal and inferred meanings and to pause and deliberate over the unfolding story. E-texts, on the other hand, are short and move back and forth quickly, habituating students to moving quickly over text rather than to slowing down and reflecting.

2. A capacity for uninterrupted thinking to maintain a train of thought and to hold enough information in working memory to understand the text. Complex texts are not constructed to allow for quick snippets of attention as they often deal with scenes and ideas not known to today's teenagers. Grasping meaning from complex tests requires single-tasking and constant focus, not the task switching and rapid and constant interaction of digital communications.

3. An openness for deep thinking that involves, for instance, deciding whether to agree or disagree with the author's premise, and reflecting on alternatives. Complex texts often cause teenagers to confront the paucity of their knowledge and the limits of their experiences. Instead of being humbled by these revelations and reading deeper, adolescents respond by accepting that the persona they have established on their personal profile pages is self-sufficient.

Bauerlein suggests that high schools devote at least one hour a day to research assignments that use print matter, require no connection to the Internet, and include complex texts. The key is not to eliminate technology, but to control its invasion into the time that should be devoted to deep thinking.

Technology is neither a panacea nor an enemy. It is a tool. Students in the primary and middle school grades still need personal contact and interaction with their teachers and peers. This is an important part of social development, but technology, perhaps to a great extent, is reducing the frequency of these interactions. We should not be providing technology for technology's sake, nor should the technology be an end unto itself. Rather than teaching with the various technologies, teachers should use them to enhance, enrich, and present their content more efficiently. Many Internet sites offer free materials to help teachers expand their lessons with audio and video pieces. See the Resources section for some suggested sites.

Have Schools Changed With the Environment?

Many educators are recognizing the characteristics of the new brain, but they do not always agree on what to do about it. Typical teenagers at home are constantly switching with ease among their MP3 player, cell phone, laptop, video games, and television. Multimedia is all around them. Can we then expect them to sit quietly for 30 to 50 minutes listening to the teacher, filling in a worksheet, or working alone? Granted, teaching methodologies are changing, and teachers are using newer technologies and even introducing pop music and culture to supplement traditional classroom materials. But schools and teaching are not changing fast enough. In high schools, lecturing continues to be the main method of instruction, primarily because of the vast amount of required curriculum material and the pressure of increased accountability and high-stakes testing. Students remark that school is a dull, nonengaging environment that is much less interesting than what is available outside school. Despite the recent efforts of educators to deal with this new brain, many high school students still do not feel challenged. In the 2009 High School Survey of Student Engagement, 65 percent of the nearly 43,000 students responded that they "like discussions in which there are no clear answers." At the same time, 82 percent said they would welcome chances to be creative in school (Yazzie-Mintz, 2010).

In another survey of 10,500 high school students, conducted by the National Governors Association (2005), more than one third of the students said their school had not done a good job challenging them to think critically and analyze problems. About 11 percent said they were thinking of dropping out of school. Over one third of this group said they were leaving because they were "not learning anything."

A 2004 Gallup poll asked nearly 800 students ages 13 to 17 in an online survey to select three adjectives that best described how they felt about school. Half the students chose *bored*, and 42 percent chose *tired*.

The Importance of Exercise. Just think about some of the things we do in schools that run counter to what we know about how the brain learns. One simple but important example is the notion of exercise. Exercise increases blood flow to the brain and throughout the body. The additional blood in the brain is particularly effective in the hippocampus, an area deeply involved in forming long-term memories. Exercise also triggers one of the brain's most powerful chemicals, a tongue twister called brain-derived neurotrophic factor (BDNF). This protein supports the health of young neurons and encourages the growth of new ones. Once again, the brain area that is most sensitive to this activity is the hippocampus. Studies show that increased physical activity in school leads to improved student performance (Taras, 2005). Yet students still sit too much in school, especially in high school, and elementary schools are reducing or eliminating recess to devote more time to preparing for high-stakes testing. In other words, we are cutting out the very activity that could improve cognitive performance on tests.

> *As we continue to develop a more scientifically based understanding about today's novel brain, we must decide how this new knowledge should change what we do in schools and classrooms.*

Clearly, we educators have to rethink now, more than ever, how we must adjust schools to accommodate and maintain the interest of this new brain. As we continue to develop a more scientifically based understanding about today's novel brain and how it learns, we must decide how this new knowledge should change what we do in schools and classrooms.

WHAT'S COMING UP?

Now that we have reviewed some basic parts of the brain, and discussed how the brain of today's student has become acclimated to novelty, the next step is to look at a model of how the brain processes new information. Why do students remember so little and forget so much? How does the brain decide what to retain and what to discard? The answers to these and other important questions about brain processing will be found in the next chapter.

PRACTITIONER'S CORNER

Fist for a Brain

This activity shows how you can use your fists to represent the human brain. Metaphors are excellent learning and remembering tools. When you are comfortable with the activity, share it with your students. They are often very interested in knowing how their brain is constructed and how it works. This is a good example of novelty.

1. Extend both arms with palms open and facing down and lock your thumbs.

2. Curl your fingers to make two fists.

3. Turn your fists inward until the knuckles touch.

4. While the fists are touching, pull both toward your chest until you are looking down on your knuckles. This is the approximate size of your brain! Not as big as you thought? Remember, it's not the size of the brain that matters; it's the number of connections between the neurons. Those connections form when stimuli result in learning. The thumbs are the front and are crossed to remind us that the left side of the brain controls the right side of the body and that the right side of the brain controls the left side of the body. The knuckles and outside part of the hands represent the **cerebrum** or thinking part of the brain.

5. Spread your palms apart while keeping the knuckles touching. Look at the tips of your fingers, which represent the **limbic** or emotional area. Note how this area is buried deep within the brain and how the fingers are mirror-imaged. This reminds us that most of the structures of the limbic system are duplicated in each hemisphere.

6. The wrists are the **brain stem** where vital body functions (e.g., body temperature, heartbeat, blood pressure) are controlled. Rotating your hands shows how the brain can move on top of the spinal column, which is represented by your forearms.

PRACTITIONER'S CORNER

Review of Brain Area Functions

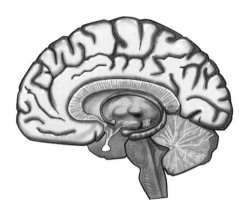

Here is an opportunity to assess your understanding of the major brain areas. Write in the table below your own key words and phrases to describe the functions of each of the eight brain areas. Then draw an arrow to each brain area on the diagram below and label it.

Amygdala:
Brain stem:
Cerebellum:
Cerebrum:
Frontal Lobe:
Hippocampus:
Hypothalamus:
Thalamus:

PRACTITIONER'S CORNER

Using Novelty in Lessons

Using novelty does *not* mean that the teacher needs to be a stand-up comic or the classroom a three-ring circus. It simply means using a varied teaching approach that involves more student activity. Here are a few suggestions for incorporating novelty in your lessons.

- **Humor.** There are many positive benefits that come from using humor in the classroom at all grade levels. See the Practitioner's Corner in Chapter 2 (p. 68), which suggests guidelines and beneficial reasons for using humor.

- **Movement.** When we sit for more than 20 minutes, our blood pools in our seat and in our feet. By getting up and moving, we recirculate that blood. Within a minute, there is about 15 percent more blood in our brain. We do think better on our feet than on our seat! Students sit too much in classrooms, especially in secondary schools. Look for ways to get students up and moving, especially when they are verbally rehearsing what they have learned.

- **Multisensory Instruction.** Today's students are acclimated to a multisensory environment. They are more likely to give attention if there are interesting, colorful visuals; if they can interact with appropriate technology; and if they can walk around and talk about their learning.

- **Quiz Games.** Have students develop a quiz game or another similar activity to test each other on their knowledge of the concepts taught. This is a common strategy in elementary classrooms but underutilized in secondary schools. Besides being fun, it has the added value of making students rehearse and understand the concepts in order to create the quiz questions and answers.

- **Music.** Although the research is inconclusive, there are some benefits of playing music in the classroom at certain times during the learning episode. See the Practitioner's Corner in Chapter 6 (p. 241) on the use of music.

PRACTITIONER'S CORNER

Preparing the Brain for Taking a Test

Taking a test can be a stressful event. Chances are your students will perform better on a test of cognitive or physical performance if you prepare their brains with one of the following:

- **Exercise.** Get the students up to do some exercise for just two minutes. Jumping jacks are good because the students stay in place. Students who may not want to jump up and down can do five brisk round-trip walks along the longest wall of the classroom. The purpose here is to get the blood oxygenated and moving faster.

- **Fruit.** Besides oxygen, brain cells also need glucose for fuel. Fruit is an excellent source of glucose. Students should eat about two ounces (more than 50 grams) of fruit each day. Dried fruit, such as raisins, is convenient. Avoid fruit drinks as they often contain just fructose, a fruit sugar that does not provide immediate energy to cells. The chart below shows how just 50 grams of glucose increased long-term memory recall in a group of young adults by 35 percent and recall from working memory by over 20 percent (Korol & Gold, 1998). Subsequent studies have found similar memory boosts (M. A. Smith, Riby, van Eekelen, & Foster, 2011; Sünram-Lea et al., 2008).

- **Water.** Wash down the fruit with an eight-ounce glass of water. The water gets the sugar into the bloodstream faster and hydrates the brain.

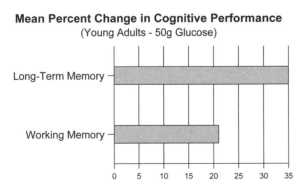

Mean Percent Change in Cognitive Performance
(Young Adults - 50g Glucose)

Wait about five minutes after these steps before giving the test. That should be enough time for the added glucose to fire up the brain cells. The effect lasts for only about 30 minutes, so the steps need to be repeated periodically for longer tests.

Chapter 1—Basic Brain Facts

Key Points to Ponder

Jot down on this page key points, ideas, strategies, and resources you want to consider later. This sheet is your personal journal summary and will help to jog your memory.

_____

_____

_____

_____

_____

_____

_____

_____

_____

_____

2

The Child's Brain

Robert Sylwester

Childhood development occurs within our entire body, but much of childhood nurturing occurs during conversations between adult and juvenile brains. A mature plant doesn't nurture its germinated seeds, however, and brainless plants are as biologically successful as animals, so what's the point of a brain?

The principal reason that animals have a brain and plants don't is because animals can move of their own volition and plants can't. Rooted plants aren't going anywhere, so they don't even need to know where they are. What's the point of knowing that other plants have better access to sunlight and water, or that a logger is approaching, if you can't do anything about it?

However, if an organism has legs, wings, or fins, it needs a sensory system to provide information about here and there, a decision-making system to determine if here is better than there or there is better than here, a motor system to get it to there if that's the better option, and a memory system to get back to here after its trip.

Here and there are about space, but our brain also needs to integrate space with time. Movement not only requires the expenditure of energy across space but also over the time it takes to plan and execute movements. Objects and events move slowly or quickly, continuously or intermittently. A brain is thus a system that uses energy to integrate space and time in the regulation of movement—and of life, for all that.

It all begins with a typically pleasant trip of a sperm in search of an egg. Nine months later, our exit trip through our mother's birth canal and the severing of our umbilical cord signal the beginning of an increasingly independent life of movement in all its glorious complexities. Our basic equipment for this journey through life is a three-part motor system—a leg/foot/toe system at the bottom that's about half our body's length and allows us to physically move from here to there and to kick things; an arm/hand/finger system in the middle that extends our reach about two feet and allows us to grasp, carry, throw, and write; and a neck/face/tongue system at the top that initiates digestion and activates a rhythmic flow of air molecules that move linguistic and musical information between and among brains.

These motor systems are excellent but finite. Humans have thus added technological extensions—such as shoes, ladders, wheels, boats, and airplanes—to increase the range and speed of our leg/foot/toe system; hammers, pliers, screwdrivers, gloves, grocery carts, guns, and pencils to increase the capabilities of our arm/hand/finger system; and knives, blenders, cooking, binoculars, microphones, and language to increase the capabilities of our neck/face/tongue system.

Much of our childhood is spent in the development and mastery of personal and technological motor skills. Children seem to intuitively know that if they hope to drive a car at 16, they better get on a tricycle at three. They have to master the integration of perception, arms, and legs in the control of wheels before their parents will give them the keys to the family car. They thus happily spend many hundreds of practice hours on bicycles and skateboards to master wheeled movement in natural space and time.

Similarly, 21st-century children seem to intuitively know that they also have to master movement in cyber space and time. Video game controls are the electronic equivalent of tricycles, and children typically begin to play with the controls of simple games at about three. They seem to realize that they have to master the finite world of game controls and children's video games before they can explore the more complex adult video games and the infinity of the Internet.

But how do children begin the process of learning the myriad of such intentional movements that they must master? For example, if a mother sticks out her tongue at her observant infant a few hours after birth, the infant will intuitively reciprocate without any conscious knowledge of what a tongue is or prior experience with the complex act of projecting a tongue.

The same is true of other early imitative behaviors, such as smiling and clapping hands. Further, many motor skills must begin to develop almost immediately, and most complex motor skills (such as tying a pair of shoes) can't be learned solely through verbal directions.

So although effective movement is our brain's defining property, much of the underlying neurobiology of its activation and mastery was an enigma until recently, when **mirror neurons** were discovered.

Mirror Neurons

Most human movement is made up of a relatively few basic motor sequences that can be differentially combined and repeated into many actions. For example, our arm reaches out as our fist opens and closes to grasp a glass of water that we then retract to our mouth and tip. As indicated in Chapter 1, language involves saying or writing specific verbal sequences, such as the letters in *dog* and *god* or the words in the sentences *Bill hit Mary,* as opposed to *Mary hit Bill.* The five-element *reach, grasp, elevate, retract, tip* motor sequence can be represented with a five-element letter sequence—*d-r-i-n-k.* The sequence of elements is central in both cases, and each basic movement or letter may be used as an element of many other actions or words.

Our brain contains myriads of **neural networks** that store and retrieve memories of general and specific facts, personal experiences, and motor sequences. We automatically execute frequently used motor sequences, such as grasping a glass, even though glass sizes differ, but we shift from such automatic behaviors to consciously executed variations if the immediate task is sufficiently different from the mastered skill.

Think of an airplane pilot, who consciously takes off and lands the plane and simply monitors flight events when the computerized automatic pilot is guiding the plane. If a weather front or some other problem arises, the pilot resumes conscious control until the problem is resolved. We often experience an analogous situation when our car is on cruise control and we're carrying on a conversation with a passenger. The conversation briefly stops when something in the road ahead suggests that we should shift from cruise to conscious control of the car and focus our attention completely on driving.

Suffice it to say at this point that several brain systems collaborate in learning, planning, and executing conscious and automatic movements. Two systems important to understanding mirror neurons and intentional movement are the **motor cortex,** which activates the specific muscles involved in a motor sequence, and the **premotor area** of the **frontal lobes**, which remembers and primes the motor sequence.

Giacomo Rizzolatti (Rizzolatti & Sinigaglia, 2007) and his team of Italian neuroscientists discovered mirror neurons in the early 1990s. They were studying the brain systems that regulate intentional hand movements in monkeys. They discovered that neurons in the premotor areas of the **cortex** that remember and prime motor sequences (such as how to grasp an object or to break open a peanut) activate milliseconds before the motor cortex neurons fire and the action occurs. The relevant premotor system thus forms an action sequence that activates the relevant motor cortex system that activates the relevant muscles.

What amazed the scientists was the discovery one day that this premotor system also activates when their monkey simply observed someone else making that same intentional movement.

These premotor neurons don't activate at the mere observation of a hand or mouth—only when it is carrying out a goal-directed action. Further, they respond to a hand but not to a tool that is grasping or moving an object because a brain's motor areas regulate body parts and not tools. When the target of an action is an object (such as picking up a peanut) certain **parietal lobe** neurons are also activated. Scientists called this system the mirror neuron system.

This discovery was very significant because it identified the brain systems that create a mental template of an observed intentional movement of someone else, and then prime the responsive imitative behavior. They don't in themselves generate the response, but rather they enhance its probability. In effect, mirror neurons connect the subjective worlds of the actor and observer.

A cognitive system that allows a brain to automatically simulate and then to imitate the observed goal-directed movements of others would thus be an ideal learning system for complex movements, and that's the critically important role that mirror neurons play in the maturation of a brain's movement capabilities.

After the initial monkey research, neuroscientists used **neuroimaging technologies** to study mirror neurons in humans. They discovered that we have an incredibly complex mirror neuron system that encompasses our entire sensory and perceptual systems, allowing us to both simulate and empathize with the emotional lives and intentional states of others, driving our rich communicative and cultural life. Mirror neurons are thus central to our very existence as a social species, because our immature birth brain must master many motor skills during childhood.

When we observe someone yawn, it activates our brain's yawning program. Adults typically override the tendency and stifle the yawn; however, as indicated above, if we stick out our tongue at an infant who is only a few hours old, it's probable that she will immediately reciprocate even though she had never before stuck out her tongue or even has any conscious awareness of it. The chances are good, however, that it's the fetal muscle she exercised the most by sucking her thumb.

Her observation of our behavior will automatically activate the mirror neurons that prime the motor neurons that activate her tongue projection movements. She has a zillion movements to learn and therefore no reason to stifle the action. Similarly, smile, and she'll smile. Clap your hands, and she'll clap her hands. The statement *monkey see, monkey do* also relates nicely to human infants.

Life would be chaotic, however, if the extended human mirror neuron system was simply a subconscious automatic system that imitated every observed intentional action. Our brain must thus rapidly determine if it's simply enough to know the state of another person (and so to stifle a yawn) or to reciprocate a movement sequence (such as when someone initiates a handshake or a hug). A common communicated understanding about what's important and appropriate must therefore exist in both the actor and the observer.

Communication. As indicated above, language is a key form of human movement. It's probable that mirror neurons helped to expand human communication from gestural to vocal sequences. We can use our legs to approach a friend and extend our hand for a handshake greeting, but we can also stay where we are and project rhythmic air patterns via mouth and tongue movements. These sequential sound patterns activate ear and brain activity that our friend interprets as a verbal greeting. Written language and music are thus also forms of communicative movement.

We can observe the friendly movements of a handshake, but we cannot see what's occurring inside a speaker's mouth, where speech sounds are regulated. The mirror neuron system helps to explain how a child learns to speak.

Our sensorimotor system is highly interconnected, so we can visualize a named but nonvisible object, such as when someone says *banana*. Similarly, hearing articulate speech activates the same speech-production processes in the child's brain that the speaker used to sequence the sounds and words. This process is enhanced through *Motherese,* a universal behavior in which an adult holds an infant in a close face-on-face position; and then speaks in a slowed-down, high-pitched, exaggerated, repetitive, melodic format that engages the infant's attention and easily activates her mirror neuron system. Speech is a complex motor activity, so the infant initially *babbles* in incoherent imitation; but, over time, in a verbal environment, the child begins to correctly utter simple phonemic combinations . . . and eventually, smooth articulate speech emerges.

We often use gestures to accompany conversational and presentational speech. The gestures supplement and enhance the meaning, rhythmic pattern, and emotional overtones of what we say. Mirror neuron involvement in the process is evident when observers overtly or covertly imitate the speaker's gestures. Mimicked gestures are also integral to many children's songs and games.

When we observe someone in the initial stages of a movement sequence, such as when a diner picks up a knife and fork, we infer the subsequent actions because our brain is *mirroring* the entire common movement sequence and so *knows* what will occur next. When a speaker stops midsentence, we can often complete the sentence.

Think of how your computer will complete a frequently used e-mail or website address after you type the first few letters. Our brain similarly remembers entire movement sequences.

This probably also explains why most people consider it more difficult to give a formal speech than to engage in a conversation. Two brains work together easily when exploring an idea conversationally. They infer, build on, and complete each other's thoughts in an informal manner that allows the conversation to meander as it will.

This ability to infer the direction of an observed behavior is also important for adults who are supervising children. When we observe a child in the initial stages of inappropriate or risky behavior, we can anticipate the probable result and intervene before it's too late.

Athletes *fake out* an opponent's mirror neuron system by beginning an action, and then quickly and unexpectedly switching to a different action. Magicians use the same switching technique to fool their audience. A continued untrue explanation may similarly place hearers into a mirrored mental state in which the deception eventually seems reasonable.

Ballroom dancing, musical duets, and tennis matches are a few of the many examples of social interaction in which partners enjoy the mirrored activity of unspoken communication.

Empathy and Compassion. Because our brain's hundreds of processing systems are highly interconnected, mirror neurons not only simulate the actions of others but also their related properties, such as the pain or pleasure that can result from an observed action. The anterior **cingulate** and **insula** are frontal lobe systems that process pain, and mirror neurons in these systems respond to the observed pain that others are experiencing (typically communicated through facial expressions and body language). This leads to empathy and compassion, essential components for successful human interaction. The term *empathy* describes our ability to internalize and so understand the emotional state of another person, and *compassion* describes the feelings we have for the plight of that person.

Empathy and compassion can further emerge through third-party reports, such as news reports of the victims of natural disasters or accidents. We will almost always instantly recall and relive any similar experience we had.

Virtuoso Performance. Mirror neurons may also help to explain why so many of us enjoy observing and predicting the movements of virtuoso athletes, dancers, and musicians. Virtuoso performances allow our mirror neuron system to mentally model (and thus enjoy) actions that we can't physically mimic at that level of performance. Mirror neurons become more active as we gradually master a skill by observing those who are better at it than we are.

Children spend a lot of time observing and imitating the actions of older children who have mastered the movements they seek to master. We often see them standing off from the action but totally engrossed in it.

Note the body language of former athletes who are observing a game—how they actively imitate the movements of the athletes playing the game, and how they can see individual movements within the complexity of the action that the rest of us don't see. Further, athletes frequently use mental imagery to enhance their performance of specific practiced movement sequences.

Metaphor. Metaphoric thought allows us to recognize common properties in seemingly dissimilar entities, such as in a brain and a computer. Because metaphor allows us to connect novel, complex, and abstract phenomena to something we already understand, it's central to such cultural elements as the arts, humanities, and religion.

Movement can also be metaphorical. No two movements are absolutely identical, but they're often sufficiently similar that we recognize classes of movements, such as shooting free throws in basketball. A fouled player can use various techniques to shoot the ball, but it's not considered a free throw if the player doesn't stand at the free throw line or shoots the ball from the free throw line during regular play. It's thus important that our brain understands the requisite properties in comparisons.

The motor skills needed to play a guitar and violin are sufficiently similar so that a person who can play one instrument has an advantage in learning the other instrument over someone who hasn't played either. It's not surprising then that mirror neurons are an element of our metaphoric capabilities.

Several brain systems are probably involved in processing metaphors, and the **angular gyrus** is a likely principal candidate. It's located at the juncture of our sight, sound, and touch processing centers, and it contains mirror neurons.

Children typically begin to explore metaphor within the context of the stories we tell them and the books that they read. For example, many fairy tales and parables contain animals and machines that exhibit human qualities, and such stories typically seek to connect imaginary events with the life of a child.

Electronic Media. The mirror neuron system evidently works best when it directly observes human behavior, but it apparently can also respond to televised and filmed human movements. This poses intriguing currently unresolved issues about the effect of the electronic depiction of violent and sexual behavior on the subsequent real-life behavior of immature observers.

Autism. It now appears that at least some people who suffer from the autism spectrum have a deficient mirror neuron system, and this would explain their inability to infer and empathize with the thoughts and behaviors of others, to comprehend metaphor and proverbs, and to easily master articulate speech. The presumed connection between the malady and mirror neurons opens up promising research possibilities into the diagnosis and eventual treatment of autism. It's also probable that other learning disabilities will also be traced to deficiencies in our mirror neuron system.

An old adage suggests that children attend more to what we do than to what we say. If so, our mirror neuron system may eventually explain the effectiveness of many traditional teaching and parenting techniques in which explicit modeling provides children with an effective behavioral pattern to follow. For example, working with children on a task such as mixing and baking a cake at home or mixing papier-mâché paste at school encourages the imitative behaviors that mirror neurons mediate.

At another level, classroom chalkboards are increasingly being replaced by newer technologies such as PowerPoint presentations. It's perhaps an inevitable change, but PowerPoint information tends to appear full blown on the screen, as opposed to the students' observation of the teacher's arm movements and body language as a diagram, algorithm, or text gradually emerges on a chalkboard or overhead screen. Some technological developments in teaching might thus diminish traditional teacher behaviors that are developmentally significant in ways that we didn't formerly realize.

Mirror neurons may thus provide us with key elements of the neurobiological base of 21st-century theories of teaching and parenting. The renowned neuroscientist V. S. Ramachandran (2006) suggested that the discovery of mirror neurons might provide the same powerful unifying framework for our understanding of teaching and learning that the 1953 discovery of DNA did for our understanding of genetics.

MASTERING MOVEMENT

An extended sheltered human maturation permits children and adolescents to gradually and informally develop competence in basic motor skills and to explore the wide variety of challenges and solutions that independent life will later present. Such learning generally emerges through various forms of *play* and *games* that continue the developmental process begun with mirror neurons. The mastery of most motor skills requires considerable practice, which must be in the form of sufficiently pleasant experiences for the child to continue doing them.

Play involves informal individual or small-group explorations of motor skills with a minimal focus on a clearly defined goal. Play has a joy about it that communicates the pure exuberance of movement for its own sake. At some developmental point, however, young people want to compare their motor and decision-making abilities with that of others, and games do that.

Games are the more-organized and typically scored comparisons of specific skills exhibited by competing individuals or teams who have the same clearly defined goal. Skilled movement involves the ability to plan actions, to regulate movements during the action, and to predict the movements of others and objects. Games typically require success in all three tasks, and these reach their peak in such events as the Olympic Games, which seek to identify the best athletes in the world in selected motor skills. It's important to note, however, that games don't necessarily involve intense physical movement. Chess is an example of a game that is more cerebral than physical in the planning, regulation, and prediction of its movements.

Children will joyfully spend much personal time and energy on play and games that challenge them to master developmentally important knowledge and skills that relate to problems that intrigue them. In this, they frequently have no conscious awareness of the developmental needs implicit in the activity. For example, the universal childhood fascination for scary stories and games is probably related to the innate need to develop and maintain the systems that process the important **emotion** of fear and its consequent behavioral response, and to develop such systems in nonthreatening settings.

Our primary emotions are fear, anger, disgust, surprise, sadness, and joy, and we can add many secondary and blended emotions to that list (such as anticipation, tension, and pride). All involve the emotionally important cognitive arousal systems that must be developed and maintained for a brain to recognize and subsequently move away from dangers and to move toward opportunities. It's a use-it-or-lose-it proposition.

Some of these emotions may not be sufficiently activated in normal life to help maintain an important but rarely used survival skill. Play and games frequently and artificially activate temporary fear (and its handmaiden, attention), however, and this may partly explain our culture's strong and enduring interest in play and games. Note how all the other emotions (and attention) play similarly key roles in play and games.

The Arts. The arts also play an important role in the development and maintenance of motor skills. We not only want to playfully explore movement, we want to move with style and grace. For example, children seek first to simply master balance and basic movements on a skateboard, but as soon as they feel confident, their interests begin to shift from using the skateboard as merely a means of transportation to the aesthetics of skateboard movement. For all practical purposes, skateboarding becomes a form of dance.

All forms of the arts involve movement, whether it's a painter moving paint to a canvas or the rhythmic beats of a drummer or the raised eyebrow of an actor. We don't merely move to move but also to add aesthetic elements to human life.

Arts experiences that interest us tend to relate to important personal concerns. They thus allow us to explore the topics in a nonthreatening play-like manner during periods when we're not actually confronted by the problem in its real form, and so they help us to develop and maintain the emotion, attention, and problem-solving systems that normally process the challenge.

Physical Education. The recent reductions in school arts and physical education programs and the resulting loss of an atmosphere of play in school are thus a biological tragedy that we'll come to regret when our society matures in its understanding of the central role that physical movement in all of its manifestations plays in the development and maintenance of a child's brain.

Indeed, Ratey (2008) reports credible research studies that indicate how an active physical exercise program can actually improve the curricular attainment and physical well-being of students. For example, the nationally recognized Naperville, Illinois, secondary school exercise program is credited with materially increasing test scores and improving the behavior of students and the culture of the school. Further, only 3% of the 19,000 students are overweight (by body mass indicator standards), as compared to 30% nationwide.

PSYCHOLOGICAL MOVEMENT

We can also think of movement within the context of psychological states, such as moving from infancy to childhood to adolescence to young adulthood to being middle aged to elderly. We move from being unemployed to employed, from unmarried to married. We shift our allegiance from one political or religious belief to another.

We tend to be fascinated by great historical movements. Immigration in its various manifestations has been a long and continuing cultural and political issue in the United States, and the Lewis and Clark Expedition sparked increased internal movement within the country. Most religions commemorate some central movement event—the departure of Adam and Eve from the Garden of Eden, the Jewish Exodus from Egypt, Mohammed's journey from Medina to Mecca, and the Mormon trek to Utah are notable examples.

Literature abounds with the stories of people moving through time and space, from the *Odyssey* to *Moby Dick* to *Harry Potter*. The broad appeal of the Harry Potter series among young people is reflective of the variety of imaginative physical and psychological movements the young characters experience.

Movement is thus a manifestation of life itself. Our bodies teem with movement, even when we think we're immobile. Our hearts are beating and blood is flowing. Our lungs are expanding and contracting. Nutrients are moving through the digestive system. Neural impulses are coursing through our brains. Viral and bacterial invaders are moving about, warily observed by our immune systems. To be perfectly still is to be completely dead.

Teachers who prefer that their students sit still and be quiet are perhaps more interested in teaching a grove of trees than a classroom of students.

The Adolescent's Brain

Sheryl G. Feinstein

Conventional wisdom about teenagers is wrong. Teenagers are not incoherent, clumsy, sex-crazed, unpredictable, irrational monsters who can't be reasoned with—they are intelligent creatures not yet accustomed to their (unevenly) burgeoning mental strengths and capabilities. Adolescence is a time of startling growth and streamlining in the brain, enabling teens to think abstractly, speak expressively, and move gracefully. Of course, they often use their newfound abilities to talk their way out of homework deadlines or concoct elaborate games to play behind teachers' backs, but it's a good start!

Did you know that . . .

- The teen brain is particularly susceptible to novelty
- ADHD is not caused by a bad student, bad parent, or bad teacher; the reason can be found in the brain
- The burst of growth in the frontal lobes means that teens overcomplicate problems, idealize the world, and say one thing while doing another
- The development of the parietal lobes helps teen athletes improve their pace and teen musicians improve their beat
- Physical movement helps the cerebellum develop, thereby helping teens improve their cognitive processing skills
- Feedback improves the brain's efficiency
- Teens crave structure and organization in spite of their attraction to novelty

The wacky and weird teenagers who filled the hallway of the high school transformed suddenly to zombies as they filed into their English class. With drooping shoulders and shuffling feet, they exchanged resigned looks and rolled their eyes knowingly at one another. They sat in the unbroken silence and waited for their student teacher to enter.

She entered the room in the same manner as her students—no welcoming smile, no friendly words. She went to the front of the class with a stiff, swift step and abruptly launched her fifty-minute lecture on punctuation. One boy leaned over to his neighbor and pleaded, "Kill me. Kill me now." The teacher lost everyone's attention by droning on and on about the various uses of the apostrophe. All around the room, students daydreamed and drifted to sleep.

ATTENTION-GETTING DEVICES

Our first objective as teachers is to capture students' attention. If we don't gain their attention, the chance that they'll learn anything is remote at best. The process of attention serves two primary purposes, the first of which is survival. The brain kept our ancestors safe by alerting them to possible hazards in their midst like strangers, thunder clouds, or wild animals. Fortunately, it is the rare occasion that survival is at stake in school. Instead, attention serves its second purpose—maintaining pleasurable feelings. The exotic girl with the pierced tongue, a double chocolate ice cream bar, and listening to rock music on the radio are pleasurable diversions for modern teenagers. So are funny stories, terrible tragedies, and the first snowfall.

The brain is bombarded with information from the senses. Everything we see, hear, touch, smell, and taste finds its way to the sensory receptors, from the clothes on your back to the beige walls of the room and the radio playing softly in the background. At the base of the brain is the brain stem, which controls involuntary actions like breathing, blood pressure, and heartbeats. Deep within the brain stem is the reticular formation, a system of neurons that gathers information from all of your senses and controls your awareness levels. Some awareness is at a conscious level (what you see and hear the teacher do and say) and some at an unconscious level (the color of the walls or the socks you are wearing). It would be impossible for the brain to consciously focus on each bit of data it receives. You may be oblivious to the feel of a baseball hat on your head while the cute girl beside you captures your full attention. Considering the immense amount of information the brain is capable of absorbing, from the spinach stuck in your teeth to the lint on your coat, we are fortunate to be able to forget most things. Otherwise, we'd overload.

Secret Revealed

No matter what you heard in the past, teens can be as interested in photosynthesis as the armpit squelches that come from the back of the classroom! The adolescent brain really does want to learn more about the world we live in and less about the student who enters the classroom to collect the attendance, but it values novelty and unpredictability. Not even a lecture and slide show about alien technology would hold your students' attention for long without these two elements!

Dr. Linda Spear (2000), a behavioral neuroscientist at Binghamton University, studies the teenage propensity for seeking novelty; she finds that the physical changes in the brain during adolescence significantly affect what appeals to teens. Fortunately, novelty and surprise can be planned for any lesson content. Instead of just lecturing about photosynthesis, work with plants and sunlamps. Instead of labeling anatomical charts, dissect a frog. Appeal directly to the teen brain's innate interest in the unexpected and enjoy a more productive classroom.

Ask a group of teenagers what they think about school and you probably won't be surprised by the answers: "Boring." "Stupid." "School sucks." Of course, friends, potential dates, lunchtime, and doodling don't bore them; the adolescent brain is fascinated by (and seeks out) novelty and emotion (Koepp et al., 1998; Spear, 2000). Sitting through classroom instruction that fails to include either is the real test of a teen's attention. Many teaching strategies and testing options have a great deal of difficulty keeping attention and arousing emotion. Worksheets require students to pay attention to something that evolution and instinct quite frankly say is irrelevant to life. Lecture, which can be an efficient way to deliver instruction, is often not emotionally charged. Objective tests, such as those in multiple-choice or true-false formats, rarely generate emotion and are extremely difficult to apply to real-world applications. Yet lecture and worksheets are dismayingly popular means of presenting content. We miss academic opportunities when we overuse strategies that neglect our emotional and cognitive constitution—two powerful memory builders.

Capturing students' attention by engaging them in feel-good experiences is good news for teachers and teens alike; everyone enjoys dwelling on the positive. People who know how to entertain an audience are almost always sure to get their educational messages across. Consider Simon, a spirited ninth grader who definitely captured his classmates' attention when he gave his presentation about a city in America. The students had already heard a dozen speeches about cities from Philadelphia to Portland

and waited politely for another colorless, note-card-heavy tale of yet another metropolis. Nonetheless, Simon strode confidently to the front of the room and began by telling the class to imagine themselves sitting in a lawn chair, gazing at mountains, and sipping a latte. "It was such a beautiful morning. Where could we be? Aspen? Salt Lake City? No, Mianus." In complete earnestness, he continued. "I suppose you're wondering what we can do for fun in Mianus, what people are like in Mianus. That's what I am here to tell you today." Every eye in the room was riveted on Simon, first in disbelief and then in hysterics. Needless to say, Simon had everyone's attention (even if he didn't have all the facts correct).

So did a physics teacher, Mr. Berndt. Mr. Berndt thrilled his students by entering their classroom one day on in-line skates. As if the novelty of skating in class weren't enough, he had brought skates for them to use, too! Soon everyone had taken turns pulling each other around the room to determine force and speed with two different masses. In a biology class, Mr. Gjornes (who is young and in exceptional shape) turned cartwheels to demonstrate the rotation of molecules. These were two classes during which no students daydreamed, no minds drifted, and every brain gave its attention to the teacher and the lesson; not only were the activities fun, they were content meaningful, too.

Attention-getting activities are not required to be amusing or participatory, however. Mr. Hoffman, a high school principal, explained how a guest speaker captivated the entire student body with a story about how his younger brother was killed by a drunk driver and finally revealed himself as the driver. The story had the students so riveted that they carried his message right into their other classes, relating his experiences to their own actions, past and future. The principal even received phone calls from parents explaining how this tale had transformed their teenagers.

Instructional Strategies

May I Have Your Attention Please?

You can only maintain student attention if you've already captured it. Introducing novelty is one way to do it, so is engaging the physical senses and arousing curiosity. Throw novelty at teens from all sides—vary the pace and tone of your voice, dress in bell-bottoms, circulate around the room, use colored chalk, bring flowers into the room, or add the scent of lemon. Incorporate all the senses in the learning adventure.

Mrs. Reynolds introduced a unit on poetry to her ninth-grade English students by speaking to the class in French. The look of amazement on students' faces made dusting off her high school French book worth the effort. Mr. Amundson strung lights around a bulletin board describing how the legislature passes a bill, literally lighting up the room (to use a sophomoric pun)! But teachers should not always be the performers. Encourage students to act in novel ways themselves. Change their seats or surprise them with a hands-on task. You could even video record them in action and have them analyze what snags their attention.

The flip side of keeping student attention is that they have an easier time watching and listening to you when there are fewer distractions in the room. Not that you should remove a single thing from the walls—but you should be aware of annoying or repetitive mannerisms you may have, such as habitual throat clearing or fidgeting with a necklace. You would hate to discover that a student chose to spend the entire period tallying how many times you tapped your pencil against the desk or said the word *okay*. This is not the attention we're striving for.

Things to Try

- Show a comic strip or a few minutes of a television cartoon to put a smile on their faces.
- Tell a riddle: How many teenagers does it take to screw in a light bulb? (One answer is one to screw in the bulb, one to hold the ladder, and one to order a pizza. You could have students take a minute or two to write their own punch lines, too.)
- Play a song from a popular CD and ask them about why they like it—inquiring about their interests will capture their attention.
- Show a video of a trendy commercial—it's the last thing they'll expect!
- Have every one of your students find a place at the board and start listing all the words that describe what they learned that week.
- Share a story from your own middle school or high school days. Students will connect with you on a personal level, and if told well, the story will draw emotion into the classroom.
- Bring in candy as a writing prompt. You could have students create metaphors for the candy out of class content while they munch and chew.
- Pass around clay, feathers, or pieces of packing foam; hands-on objects arouse curiosity and activate the tactile senses.
- Move the location of your desk periodically. In fact, move everything periodically. Change not just students' seats but also the actual desk arrangement a few times a year.
- Mix it up; occasionally have students stand up to deliver important information or respond to key ideas.
- Read a poem by Shel Silverstein or Emily Dickinson to set a mood and engage emotions.
- Start a service project for immigrant adolescents in your community. The opportunity to contribute directly toward helping a peer is meaningful, specific, and unique. The idea will pique their interest at the very least.
- Surprise them with a celebration for work well done. Make popcorn or roller-skate on the blacktop!

ATTENTION-DEFICIT/ HYPERACTIVITY DISORDER (ADHD)

The subject of attention has particular significance for students who have attention-deficit/hyperactivity disorder (ADHD). These students are a challenge to themselves, their parents, and their teachers. Known for being distracted, impulsive, and argumentative, they lack the very cornerstones of what is needed to succeed in the classroom.

Lack of focus is one of the major obstacles students with ADHD face; it negatively impacts every aspect of their lives: academics, friendships, extracurricular, and jobs. Teachers often hear the constant refrain "I don't know" to every question posed. Where is your homework? I don't know. Why are you wandering the room? I don't know. What are you talking to her for? I don't know. This frustrating chant manifests their inability to focus.

Hyperactivity is also associated with ADHD, causing these students and everyone around them grief. Continually wired, teachers often describe the behavior of students with ADHD as "he is literally bouncing off the wall," "he can't sit still, he blurts out answers," and "he doesn't listen, he never pays attention."

Recognizing cause and effect constitutes another challenge for the student with ADHD. While most teenagers are beginning to understand that if they turn their homework in on time they learn more, have better grades, and have less stress in their lives, the teen with ADHD misses the connection.

Hyperfocusing is also a featured attribute of students with ADHD. The activity that triggers hyperfocusing is usually one that requires quick, spontaneous responses. Computer games are the perfect vehicle for this ride. Once something has caught their attention and manages to keep their attention, they are not about to put on the brakes. Interrupting a student with ADHD when they are hyperfocusing is a sure recipe for a meltdown.

Brain differences are abundant between individuals with ADHD and those without. Brain size is about three to four percent smaller in teenagers with ADHD compared to their age-mates. Fortunately, the difference in brain size in no way impacts their intelligence. Other brain differences include the basal ganglia, a part of the brain associated with thinking and emotion, and the frontal lobes, the thoughtful, decision-making center of the brain. Both have reduced activity. This affects their ability to pay attention and control their emotions. Dopamine only adds fuel to the confusion. Dopamine transporters take on too much dopamine before they pass it between brain cells; this

Instructional Strategies

- Reduce distractions—seat them near the front of the room, clear their desks of objects, and keep their desks away from high traffic areas.
- Give directions one step at a time.
- Allow frequent participation and, if possible, movement.
- Break down objectives and assignments into small segments.
- Use computer-based instruction; it will draw their attention.
- Help their disorganized minds become organized by using planners and directly teaching study skills.
- If they act inappropriately and will not control themselves, remove them from the classroom.
- Reset your expectations: don't be shocked by explosive, unacceptable behavior.
- Stay calm, because they won't. Their lack of self-control means as adults we must have more control.
- Don't engage in an argument when they are out of control.
- Supply accurate information to parents and physicians as to behaviors seen in the classroom. Because of the behavior expectations in school, we are an important part of putting the puzzle together.

misstep further affects attention and impulse control (Bloom, Beal, & Kupfer, 2006).

THE FOREST OR THE TREES?

The frontal lobes are located in the front of the brain and are the largest part of the cortex. Positioned right behind the forehead, they are responsible for cognitive processing. Speaking, reading, writing, math, and music are all processed in the frontal lobes, along with the ability to analyze, apply, and evaluate. Secondary educators are constantly contemplating how to engage students in higher-order thinking, how to start their cognitive gears turning, and how to activate their frontal lobes. Fully understanding the maturation process during adolescence paves the way for compatible instruction. Neuroscience has allowed us the opportunity to witness the dramatic changes in the frontal lobes between childhood, adolescence, and adulthood.

Figure 3.1   Human Brain

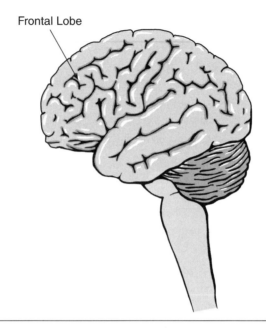

Frontal Lobe

SOURCE: Adapted from Sousa, D. A. (2003), *How the Gifted Brain Learns*, p. 16.

Children look at the world very concretely. When visiting an elementary school, I overheard a group of kindergartners trying to decide who was older between a husband and wife. It was obvious to me at first glance that the husband was older, but the kindergartners gave it an interesting twist. Lety ended the discussion by announcing, in a tone denoting the obviousness of the statement, "She's taller, so she must be the oldest." The children in attendance agreed; Lety's logic apparent to everyone. Later that day, their teacher, Ms. Gibbons, gathered all her students at the front of the room and announced that it was Presidents' Day. "Whose birthdays do we celebrate on Presidents' Day?" she asked. No one responded, so Ms. Gibbons said, "One person is Abraham Lincoln." A hand immediately shot up from the back of the group and Micah hopefully inquired, "Did he bring cupcakes?" Innocent and sweet? Absolutely. But surviving in a concrete world has its limitations. Young children have no sense of the past: Abraham Lincoln is alive, butterflies don't come from caterpillars, and monsters really do live under the bed. Adult brains are necessary to guide and structure the lives of children; they need our fine-tuned frontal lobes to shelter them.

Secret Revealed

 For years, adults have assumed that teenagers are self-absorbed, uncaring, and oblivious to the world around them. Meanwhile, teens have always been certain that they could solve all the world's problems if their stupid parents would only give them a chance. They would never allow the planet to become so polluted; they would never put an extra refrigerator in the garage when so many people are starving! If teens were in charge, all beaches would be clean and there'd be sports drinks for everyone. The world would be a better place.

As the frontal lobes mature, teens are increasingly capable of moral reasoning and idealism. Children's brains may think only in the concrete—Did I get as many cookies as she did?—but adolescence is when the brain's awareness and interest expands. Able to imagine the thoughts of another person and to appreciate the passage of time, teens suddenly become aware that they are not the only people in the world and that actions can have future consequences. They see the world not only as it is but how it could be.

The frontal lobes that distinguish men and women from boys and girls begin to mature during adolescence (Giedd, Blumenthal, Jeffries, Castellanos, et al., 1999). Young teenagers begin to think abstractly and become capable of pondering concepts that have little or no basis in concrete reality. Teens can consider hypothetical questions like "If there are millions of plants found in the rain forests, and if the majority of medicines that are discovered come from plants found in the rain forests, what implications does the deforestation of the rain forests have for our future?" They can embark on discussions ranging from civil rights to the death penalty. Teenagers can analyze, deduce, and make reflective decisions.

Educators know that secondary students need exposure to higher-level thinking skills, but the role of physical development cannot be overstated. It is the combination of biological maturation with thoughtful instructional strategies that creates a better brain. To compare teenagers to computers, we can expose teenagers to all the software we want, but until their "hard drives" are upgraded, it will have minimal impact (Epstein, 2001). "Software" that reinforces the acquisition of abstract thinking skills includes exploring various hypothetical questions, teaching broad concepts, and encouraging scientific reasoning and reflective decision making. Mostly, though, the best way to wait out this period of development is with patience and understanding. The great city of Rome wasn't built in a day, and neither is the teenage brain.

Neuroscientists and educational psychologists concur that not all teenagers develop the capacity for abstract thought at the same time. Concrete learning strategies are still needed at the middle school and high school level (Neimark, 1975). Pierre van Heile, who designed the model of geometric thought, did valuable research in teaching geometry at the high school level (Mason, 1998). He found that many older students still require concrete, hands-on material when initially studying geometry. Teacher expectations were that high school students could handle the complex and often-unfamiliar material without the support of hands-on activities. The result was student frustration and failure in this subject area.

Providing hands-on materials enabled students to quickly transition into abstract thought in geometry. This same premise is true in other areas of the curriculum. Shawna, a vivacious tenth grader, said, "My history teacher just lectures, which is not a good style for me. I daydream in that class. I try not to, but I always do. In biology class, my teacher has us doing things. One week we dissected fetal pigs. It smelled, but it made it easy to understand the parts of the body. I think I finally figured out the different ventricles in the heart." For Jason, a thoughtful boy of seventeen, concrete examples made all the difference in his understanding of upper level math. He commented, "I like my math class. We don't just do worksheets or listen to the teacher talk; we get to actually work with objects. Sometimes I need to see it to understand it."

BRUSH OFF OLD CLASSROOM FAVORITES

Some of the most traditional lesson elements are well researched and brain friendly. Robert Marzano (Marzano, Pickering, & Pollock, 2001) and his team at McREL (Mid-continent Research for Education and Learning) have led educators to institute ten nonnegotiable strategies in their classrooms. Incorporating some of these following activities will give teens the chance to practice their burgeoning ability to think abstractly while still grounding them firmly in concrete facts and information.

1. *Ask students to write a summary of a lesson.* Despite its reputation, the act of summarizing requires students to delete, substitute, and retain knowledge as they analyze information. Sifting through information during and at the end of a lesson increases their understanding of it—and it doesn't always have to happen in paragraph form. Have students directly connect five concepts that they learned that day in class, write a newspaper headline for what was covered, make a prediction about what they'll learn in the next day's class, or bring technology into the forum; have

them text message a summary. Cell phones aren't a prerequisite (they just add to the ambiance); the text can be written on a sheet of paper.

2. *Identify similarities and differences.* The brain stores by similarity, but retrieves through differences. This is another simple activity that has been shown to increase academic achievement on standardized tests. Higher-order thinking is required to compare and classify information; students must analyze and evaluate information before they can categorize it. Venn diagrams, matrix, and charts add a supportive visual to the process.

Figure 3.2   Venn Diagram

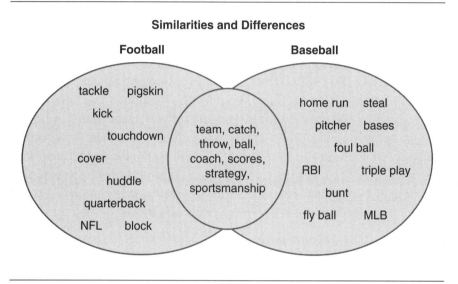

3. *Write metaphors and analogies.* Writing metaphors and analogies is an effective way to engage higher-order thinking skills. Imagine how many ways there are to fill in the blanks of the sentence: Adolescents are like _____ because _____. When given this assignment, one veteran teacher wrote, "Adolescents are like TV shows because sometimes you thoroughly enjoy them and other times you wonder who produced them." Students might enjoy filling in the blanks of a sentence like "The Internet is to _____ as the brain is to _____."

4. *Present material nonlinguistically.* Knowledge is stored in two ways, visually and linguistically. Incorporate both for optimal learning. Embracing graphic organizers, body movements, and multiple intelligences will form a firm foundation.

5. *Create and test a hypothesis.* Challenge students to apply their knowledge. Generating a hypothesis, a part of the inquiry process, helps

build a better brain. Examine water quality in school, healthy lifestyles of freshman versus seniors, or ways to make your school more Green. Amazingly, it does not matter if the answer is discovered; the journey is what matters, not the destination.

6. *Reinforce effort and provide recognition for accomplishments.* Make the connection between effort and achievement, show examples of people who overcame the odds, and inspire students to do the same. All the while, praise them for their effort and for taking that risk. Intrinsic, intrinsic, intrinsic—when it comes to recognition, replace the rewards of candy and stickers with feelings of accomplishment, and at the same time build a positive self-concept.

7. *Assign homework and provide practice.* Repeating skills helps them stick in memory. Refiring synapses strengthens the memory and makes it easier to recall; homework provides that memory-producing practice. Homework may take various forms: memorization (ribosomes, cytoplasm, proteins = Robots Can Produce), prep for the next day (read Chapter 2), understanding complex content (compare and contrast energy sources), and increasing speed (flash cards), all valuable avenues for practice. Difficulty in content and time spent on homework should increase with age; remember the fourteen-year-old brain does not have the same capabilities as the seventeen-year-old brain. Interestingly, parental assistance should be kept to a minimum; homework is no time for them to hover.

8. *Facilitate cooperative learning.* In the process, support positive interdependence. Keep the groups small and vary the composition; no one wants to always be in the "average" or the "at-risk" group. Webquests—inquiry-based Internet activities—add novelty to this first-class strategy.

9. *Set objectives and provide feedback.* Teacher objectives help set the direction of learning; when students personalize those objectives, ownership occurs. Long-term and short-term objectives, both have a place in the classroom. Feedback resets the direction of learning, immediate and specific is most effective.

10. *Start and reinforce lessons with cues, questions, and advance organizers.* Begin class on the right foot, jog their memory with questions and advance organizers. Focus on what's most important: Don't confuse the issue with trivia; they'll flounder sifting through the muck. While details may be the spice of life (goats in Morocco can climb trees), they shouldn't be the main course. Inspire students to analyze, instead of merely reacting to or describing a situation, by asking questions that force them to view a scenario in a new light. Try "How did you do that?" "What would you do differently next time?" "Why did you make that choice?" "What evidence

substantiates your conclusion?" and "What did you learn that you could apply in another class?" And remember to use wait time, the added return in quality answers is well worth your patience.

Instructional Strategies

I Think (and Solve and Inquire), Therefore I Learn

When choosing strategies, it is important to remember three things about the brain: It is capable of multiprocessing, it thrives on challenges, and it makes synapses when actively involved with learning. Instructional strategies that provide complex thinking skills and interaction provide opportunities for the brain to work more efficiently.

Take advantage of the adolescent's new ability to think abstractly by introducing a thinking curriculum into the classroom. Challenge students with assignments that promote higher-level thinking skills, such as problem-based learning, research projects, experimentation, inquiry, authentic data analysis, persuasive writing, presentations, dramas, composing music (even in a nonmusic class), and visual analysis. One day, have the students guess the legal consequences of keeping marijuana in their locker or painting graffiti or gang signs on the bathroom wall; the next day, invite a lawyer or police officer to the class to explain the actual consequences. Create a political comic book, look for a philosophy of life in popular songs, analyze a TV show or discuss hot topics like dating, parents, sex, drinking, drugs, friends, and work.

Things to Try

- Develop a new strategy for the football team or an election campaign for the candidate running for student counsel. Data mining information from the computer to solve these problems reinforces the positive use of technology.
- Think out loud for your students—verbally go through your thoughts as you decide on a topic for a writing assignment or solve a problem in trigonometry.
- Simulate a crime and investigate it; the continual popularity of this type of TV programming will grab the interest of wannabe detectives.
- Form pairs or small groups and put the students in charge. Let them teach their classmates; reciprocal teaching is one good formula for letting them shine.
- Rewrite a scene from Shakespeare against a modern day setting. Then, identify and explain similarities and differences between the two versions.
- Seek out members of the community: Interview employers about hiring adolescent workers, talk to the elderly for their historical perspective of an important event, or shadow a state legislator or city council member.

(Continued)

(Continued)

- Tap into the multiple intelligences of your students: Chart birth rates in the United States or on each continent, listen to and write about bird songs, invent a game, or visit a museum.
- View political debates on television and analyze them; watch fifteen minutes of local news and identify which issues are most likely to affect teenagers; write about contemporary concerns like forest fires, combating terrorism, stem cell research, or the use of steroids by athletes; or search the Internet to identify topics of immediate importance.
- Have students write and distribute a survey to their schoolmates (perhaps about the effect of sports programs on school spirit or academic achievement—something of significance in their lives), and collect and analyze the data.
- Develop a game of chance, like a lottery or raffle, for a charitable cause. Predict earnings and run a simulation of the game.
- Publish a class newspaper from a contemporary (what would biologists want to subscribe to?), historical (during World War I), or fictional perspective (what might Jane Eyre read?). Write engaging headlines and lead stories, draw comic strips, provide entertainment reviews, and include a financial page and advice column.
- Foreign language teachers: Have students study a country and collect information about it for the purpose of writing a tourist guide.
- Middle school teachers: Collaborate on a thematic unit. Host a Renaissance fair, sponsor an archeological dig, or investigate garbage in the community.

MAKING THE WORLD A BETTER PLACE

Abstract thought is not the only change observable in the adolescent as the frontal lobes bloom. With cognitive maturation emerges idealistic behavior; teenagers are finally able to understand the way the world works as well as envision the possibilities of an ideal place. During this stage, adolescents can become very critical of past generations (in particular, their parents' generation). In middle school, this behavior often manifests only in verbal statements—kids will talk a good game but rarely follow it up with action. For all of Jordan's arguments about the need to recycle and Kajia's concerns about the ways girls are portrayed in the media, fervent words are probably the most they will contribute to the cause. Expect even the most environmentally conscious thirteen-year-old to be assigned school ground cleanup duty for littering at least once!

As they enter high school, teens often turn idealism into activism. Older teenagers may become absorbed in service clubs that meet a variety of real-world needs, such as helping the elderly reset their clocks to daylight savings time, tutoring young children, or participating in a local walk-a-thon. Lars volunteers weekly at the local soup kitchen. He commented, "I feel really good, like I'm making a difference, helping out a lot of less-fortunate people." Mark teaches religious school to second and third graders. "I do it for community service and to help teach youth in my temple about Judaism. I enjoy it because I like working with the kids and I feel good about it because I give them a good role model. Even though they may not appreciate it or show it now, I think they'll remember my positive influence later."

But it is not uncommon for the young adolescent to be somewhat hypocritical in their idealistic behavior. They often have a difficult time practicing what they preach. David Elkind (1978) identified this characteristic as "adolescent hypocrisy" and linked it to intellectual immaturity, as opposed to a character flaw. In the context of brain development, their hypocritical behavior parallels the frontal lobe development and myelin enveloping the frontal lobes as the adolescence matures. The brain is not yet a smooth, paved road—there are still plenty of potholes, dirt paths, and back alleys to even out.

Anita spent hours telling her friends how important honesty was to her and how she would never lie to them. But when her mother asked her with whom she was going to the movies, she conveniently neglected to mention any of the boys' names. Lindsey, Kelsey, and Maggy all joined SALSA (Serve & Learn Student Association), a group committed to service. They talked excitedly about their first project, a highway cleanup south of town, sure that it was a chance to make a real difference in their community. The girls made detailed plans for the day: who would drive them there, what grubby clothes to wear, and what to put in their sack lunches. Yet Maggy's mother—who drove—was perplexed by their behavior. When asked how the day went, she replied, "The girls worked hard and had a lot of fun, but I don't understand teenagers. After picking up trash for two hours in the hot sun, we stopped for a snack; when they were finished eating, the girls left their candy wrappers on the ground! What were they thinking?"

Pseudostupidity is another educational psychology term that describes the transitioning adolescent brain (Elkind, 1978). With the development of the frontal lobes, teens are able to look at a problem from a number of perspectives. No longer is there just one correct answer; instead, they can imagine all kinds of possibilities. It sounds wonderful, but instead of simplifying their lives, it complicates them. Faced with a problem, they will think and think and think, unable to give any answer—not because it is too difficult to solve but because they have made the problem too complex. The answer may be right in front of their noses but they concentrate on every possible solution rather than an obvious one.

Mr. Armstrong, a middle school math teacher, assigned a simple assignment as homework. Students were to use toothpicks to show how one aspect of geometry (exponential growth) worked. All the assignment required was toothpicks, paper, and glue. What could be easier than doubling one toothpick to a group of two, the group of two to a group of four, four to eight, and so on? By doing the assignment, students would learn just how fast exponential growth took place. At 9:30 that evening, Mr. Armstrong received a phone call from a frantic parent whose sixth-grade son, Sam, was in tears. Sam was sure he needed to demonstrate the complexities of the geometric system to the hundredth degree; the family didn't have anywhere near enough toothpicks in the house, and the drugstore was closed. Somehow, in this student's mind, the project had become much more complex than what had been assigned.

Pseudostupidity also appears in social settings. A simple request to hang up a coat in the closet can set the adolescent mind running amuck: "Are they trying to control me? If I refuse am I just doing it because I think they are trying to control me when they aren't? What should I do?" Usually what a teenager does is get mad. An innocent remark becomes fuel for a teenage conflagration—or for a teenage anxiety attack: Amanda, a very likable teenager, was worried about making friends after her family moved to a new school district. One of her teachers reported that she went to extremes to get classmates to like her—brought them treats, agreed with everything they said, just wore herself out to get noticed—when all she really had to do was be herself.

Instructional Strategies

Walking the Walk: Countering Teenage Hypocrisy

The best way to counter teenage hypocrisy is to immerse them in the real world and in their community. Exposing adolescents to the way things really work and showing them real-life consequences to their behavior will help make the connection between well-intentioned words and meaningful actions.

- Have students research service agencies and volunteer in the community at soup kitchens or shelters, act as mentors to younger children, or participate in diversity projects.

- Encourage students to offer help on a local political campaign.
- Invite people from the community—an elderly veteran, a local artist, someone who trains Seeing Eye dogs, anyone of interest—to be guest speakers in your class.
- Enact historical or government simulations.
- Compare the experiences of characters on television or in books to the real lives of students.
- Take a trip to a city dump or landfill and talk about recycling and littering on your campus.
- Attend cyberschool—investigate controversial issues on the Internet and discuss how they impact your thinking. Stimulate the conversation further by figuring out solutions. Channel that adolescent energy into positive action.

Secret Revealed

It may come as some surprise for parents to learn that teenagers aren't claiming the garage for rock band practice just to give them a headache. Research has discovered the real reason behind the sudden enthusiasm for this noisy pastime—the parietal lobes are in full bloom! Suddenly, kids who grumbled about practicing for weekly music lessons can't get enough of playing the guitar or singing into a microphone. Kids who grumbled when Saturday morning cartoons ended now "waste" the day shooting hoops or hitting a tennis ball against the front of the house.

The parietal lobes control our sense of spatial awareness and the fluidity of the body's movements. Teen brains are busy forming new neurons and cleaning up old synaptic connections, fine-tuning adolescents' control over their fingers, arms, and legs. Their interest in all things physical springs from the discovery that, for the first time, they can actually play that tricky chord pattern and predict where that fly ball is going to land. Practice finally is likely to make perfect—the extra effort pays off, and everything is so much more fun.

BACKSTAGE IN THE THEATER OF THE TEEN MIND

The parietal lobes are located at the top of the brain toward the back of each hemisphere. The front and back areas of the parietal lobes each have separate jobs. The front part receives messages from our senses, like pain, pressure, and temperature. Am I cold? Do I need a jacket? Are these pants too tight? Information from all over the body is sent here and then monitored. Not all areas of the body are represented equally, however; the lips and tongue are particularly sensitive to outside stimulus and have extensive network access to the parietal lobes. The back part of the parietal lobes is responsible for logic and spatial awareness and keeps track of where our fingers, feet, and head are in relation to our surroundings. They keep the rhythms of our motions going and help us avoid that clumsy misstep.

Figure 3.3 Human Brain

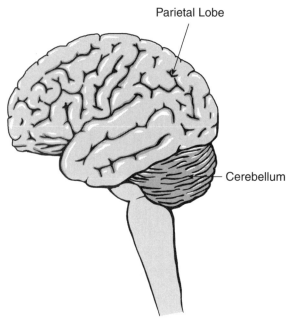

SOURCE: Adapted from Sousa, D. A. (2003), *How the Gifted Brain Learns*, p. 16.

Because early adolescence is when the parietal lobes create gray matter and prune extraneous neurons, it is a critical time for learning. As the parietal lobes mature, the ability to become proficient in sports and musical instruments is particularly enhanced. Caitlin, a track star, exudes enthusiasm as she completes the mile five seconds faster than her personal best. Wyatt practices the piano, playing with an ease and grace that is appreciated by everyone within earshot. Both of these individuals made huge strides in their capabilities during their teenage years.

We see this growth in athletics all the time. The junior varsity basketball team may have a tough time competing against the varsity team today, but the younger athletes keep practicing and learning the plays; next year, they'll be the ones playing varsity. Ninth-grade teachers are probably the most familiar with this transformation—their students go from confused, intimidated, and naïve in September to confident by May. The ninth-grade boy who spent the whole year with all his textbooks in his backpack (because he was too embarrassed to ask for help locating his locker) casually approaches the principal to discuss a class change in tenth grade.

"EVERY MOVE YOU MAKE, EVERY STEP YOU TAKE . . ."

The cerebellum, located at the back of the brain, looks like a head of cauliflower and has more neurons than any other area of the brain. It is another part of the brain associated with movement. It is particularly linked to balance, posture, and gross motor skills like riding a bike, jogging, or snapping your flip-flops. It does not reach maturation until young adulthood, and its greatest changes happen during adolescence. Although Sting, the lead singer of the band The Police, may not have been referring to the cerebellum with his lyrics, "every move you make, every step you take, I'll be watching you," they certainly apply—the cerebellum guides and modifies our every action! But neuroscience has recently revealed that the cerebellum is also involved in the coordination of cognitive processes. It actually makes thinking tasks easier. Just as it balances and guides our physical movement, it keeps our thought processes moving smoothly. The more complicated a task facing us, the larger the role the cerebellum plays in resolving it (Giedd, Blumenthal, Jeffries, Castellanos, et al., 1999).

Secret Revealed

Maybe we shouldn't have been making jokes about "dumb jocks" for all these years. Have you ever noticed how complicated a football playbook is? Could you memorize all those diagrams and recall them during the stress of competition? New research reveals that physical fitness might be what helps football players keep it in their heads! Dr. Jay Giedd (Giedd, Castellanos, Rajapakse, Vaituzis, & Rapoport, 1997), the neuroscientist from the National Institute of Mental Health (Remember him from Chapter 1?), also discovered that the

(Continued)

(Continued)

cerebellum, so long considered the "motor center" of the brain, plays a crucial role in coordinating thought processes and making decisions, too.

Teens need to move! Contradictory though it may seem, cutting PE and intramural sports is not the right way to improve academic programs at schools. A strong cerebellum is essential for efficient problem-solving skills and mental planning. Without regular physical activity, the teen brain gets the signal that the neurons in the cerebellum aren't as important as the neurons in other places (and less important neurons are in danger of being pruned). And without a strong and healthy cerebellum, that multistep math problem and reflective essay are much harder to do.

The cerebellum works in coordination with the motor cortex. When the cortex decides at a conscious level to move, it relays a message to the cerebellum. The cerebellum is connected by neurons to all the muscles in the body; it calculates which muscles are needed to enact the motion, sends them the message to move, and off you go! The cerebellum then continues to monitor and make adjustments to your movements. No wonder some people find it difficult to walk and chew gum at the same time! The combination requires the cerebellum to control two completely different sets of muscle groups.

Just as the abilities to play soccer, dance, or walk to school are guided by the cerebellum, so seem to be the thinking skills involved in planning a party, organizing a research paper, or making a reflective decision (Giedd, Blumenthal, Jeffries, Castellanos, et al., 1999). Your ability to read (although not your ability to comprehend) is stored in the cerebellum, as are song lyrics and lines from favorite movies ("Here's lookin' at you, kid") (Leonard, 1999). Like learning physical skills, the adolescent needs opportunities to practice cognitive processes in order to improve them. Teachers who involve students in thinking skills will help their students' cerebellums refine processing skills. Adolescents involved in bodily kinesthetic movement, whether taking part in a structured physical education class, participating in extracurricular activities, or playing musical instruments, will strengthen the neural connections in their adolescent cerebellum. Use it or lose it applies to the neurons in the cerebellum as much as the neurons in the cortex; they are all strengthened or sacrificed depending on usage.

Sadly, participation in all types of physical activity declines as children advance through school; maintaining moderate activity levels is a greater challenge for the adolescent than the child. As districts face financial challenges, physical education graduation requirements are being reduced throughout the country. For example, districts that once required one credit of physical education for graduation are now considering reducing the requirement to one-half credit. Although most schools still maintain afterschool sports programs and individual students exercise during their (ever-diminishing) free time, the lack of formal physical education classes will ultimately affect student cognition as well as coordination.

It is known that the adolescent who engages in challenging cognitive activities increases and strengthens the neurons involved in coordinating thinking skills (Giedd, Blumenthal, Jeffries, Castellanos, et al., 1999). Actively involving students with brain-compatible learning strategies, such as art or science projects, simulations, and problem-solving activities, will build better cerebellums than will forcing students into the roles of consistently passive recipients of knowledge. Elementary school teachers commonly use body movements to support learning, but secondary teachers aren't always comfortable with such techniques. Even though their students say things like "A math teacher had us move to learn a theorem—it was helpful," and "In our American Studies class, the teacher had guys act out the characters of different stories. I can still see how they did it!"

Interestingly, the cerebellum is the area of the brain that differs the most between teenage boys and girls. Cerebellums in adolescent boys are about fourteen percent larger than cerebellums in adolescent girls, and the difference remains through adulthood (Raz, Gunning-Dixon, Head, Williamson, & Acker, 2001). It is speculated that the difference between male and female cerebellum size is partially a result of human evolution—males were the ones tracking and hunting while females were the ones keeping the home fires burning. Because the cerebellum controlled the skills the males were using, they developed larger cerebellums. (In general, the size of any brain component is proportionate to the amount of processing it does.) Whether or not this supposition is true, a larger cerebellum may explain why the boys in your class like to be in motion (moving their legs and stretching their arms) and the girls don't mind sitting and listening. Boys and girls both benefit, however, from the cognitive skills that come from physical movement.

Instructional Strategies

Of Sound Mind and Body

An extensive study of the benefits of active learning was done in elementary and middle schools in Chicago. Classrooms that actively engaged students were compared to classrooms that viewed students as passive receptors, relying on drill and practice to increase learning. The results were impressive. Classrooms that had a great deal of interaction and didactic instruction saw dramatic increases in scores on the Iowa Test of Basic Skills in reading and math over a four-year period (Smith, Lee, & Newmann, 2001).

Active learning doesn't come without challenges: Limited class time, greater prep time, lack of materials, and of course the biggest challenge of all—the possibility that students won't engage, are some of the issues teachers face. Give yourself a break; remember that while creative methods of urging participation are great, simply mixing lecture and discussion creates an actively involved classroom. Whatever method you use to actively engage students, the payback in academic achievement is worth taking the risk.

Teachers come to the same conclusion informally all the time. Mr. Miller, a high school math teacher, was concerned that year after year his students had difficulty understanding the concept of slope. He decided to see if active learning in place of paper and pencil exercises would make a difference. "I had them measuring the slope on the school's handicapped accessible ramps, the football field, and the staircases. I know I had a lot of fun, and I think they did, too. The best news was that their tests showed they had a much better understanding of slope when all was said and done." Active learning works.

So incorporate movement into learning—sit less and move more. Enact simulations, play charades, and do energizers. Choreograph body movements to represent phenomena in nature or the emotions of a character in literature. Allow students to step into the psyche of a new character. Let them act out the experience of being a boring guest speaker, substitute teacher, or the teacher arguing with a student over a grade by stepping into another person's shoes. Compose a song. Create a collage, time capsule, or board game. Conduct a science experiment. Get out the cotton swabs, construction paper, marshmallows, and toothpicks and get busy!

Things to Try

- Have students create time capsules of their lives. "Bury" the collective contributions somewhere on campus (in a safe place) and open them a year or two later. Then, let students take their individual capsules home. The personal connection at both ends of the project will engage all students.
- Simulate a mock Congress. Having representatives from every state will involve every student. Students work individually to gather data but work collectively to present it.
- Make a board game about some lesson in a social studies, English, or math class. Have students exchange games and play them. Small groups of students will form naturally; designing the games is educational, but playing them is fun.

- Design a bumper sticker that reflects political views on an issue—this activity combines creativity with academic research. Have a contest with silly prizes for the best bumper stickers in a variety of categories, such as "Bumper Sticker that Will Fit on the Smallest Car."

- Tour and study historic buildings in your area. Not only will a field trip give students a sense of perspective about their community and times gone by, the novelty of the location will make a better background against which to remember new knowledge. The effort of walking through rooms or from building to building will engage the cerebellum.

- Create a collage from recycled materials. This hands-on project allows students to communicate their ideas about real-world issues while expressing themselves artistically.

- Create an advertisement for nutritional eating. Higher-level thinking is engaged as students analyze and decide what information is most important for consumers to know, what will grab their attention, and how to get the message across.

- Make a brochure of your life, school, or community. Who are you? What do you stand for? Choose an audience of peers, parents, teachers, or community. Ask students to discuss how their brochures could change to suit different audiences.

- Teach a lesson in television-talk-show or trivia-game-show format. Students can write questions and keep score. They can also take turns playing host and guests or game participants—and so can you!

- For physical education teachers: Have students design and implement a personal fitness program after assessing personal strength, endurance, and flexibility. Teens will practice setting goals, compete with themselves instead of each other (promoting camaraderie and cooperation), and benefit from improved physical health.

- Research a need in the community, hypothesize a solution, and propose it to the local school board. Not only would students have to think abstractly, they would also have the chance to offer their knowledge to the community. Making a real contribution is a motivator and a true self-esteem builder.

FEEDBACK: FOOD FOR LEARNING

The brain works via a system of checks and balances. It chooses its next cognitive move on the basis of what it just did (Bangert-Drowns, Kulik, Kulik, & Morgan, 1991). Feedback is required to clarify and correct the information we receive; it allows the brain to readjust and reevaluate what it thinks it knows. Feedback is best when it is corrective in nature, explaining what students did right and wrong. Positive feedback—which can include suggestions about how to improve or change—helps us cope with stress. Our adrenal system goes into overdrive when we are stressed; hearing the words "That's right," "Good job," or "Nice work" keeps us relaxed.

Secret Revealed

 It's time for teachers to reconsider everything they've thought about giving feedback to students. Teens don't crave feedback because they are insecure about their academic performance or needy for attention—they crave feedback because it helps them finish learning. Learning, the growth of new neurons and the creation of new synaptic connections, is the brain's response to stimulus. Stimulus, response, stimulus, response—responding to environmental stimulus is one of the basic life functions. Externally, we respond to rain by seeking shelter and to hot stoves by pulling our hand away. Internally, we respond to hunger by eating and to germs by activating the immune system—and by restructuring the brain according to knowledge we acquire.

Feedback is one form of stimulus. When the brain gets no stimulus of feedback, it has no reason to respond to information by learning. Feedback is especially important to teenagers because of the changes occurring in their brain. Without information about their performance, their brains won't know what neurons to grow or which ones to prune. Positive feedback actually releases serotonin into the brain, reinforcing feelings of calm and happiness. Feedback, in the classroom and in life, is one of the most important ways you can help teens turn their brains into efficient learning systems.

Feedback is especially important during adolescence, when the brain is undergoing so much building and pruning of synapses. Rarely do students understand things the first time they are presented; the brain learns through trial and error. As their brains take in new information, certain neurons are activated and certain neurons are not. Feedback is just as important as the original information sent to the brain because it completes the cycle of learning. Feedback helps teen brains decide which neurons to turn on and which to turn off, assisting the brain in making adjustments and correcting misinformation. The brain tries one combination and then another until the correct response is learned (and probably does more eliminating than increasing of neuron activity).

Feedback must be timely and specific to be of any use. Consider Lee, who was frustrated and disgusted with his English teacher. "The whole semester we only did one paper, at the beginning of the year, and we didn't get it back until finals. My paper just had one large B on the front—no other comments. It was really stupid. She hardly had anything to grade our writing on, and we never got a chance to improve." Worst-case scenario, sure, but returning work in an untimely fashion is a recurring theme in some classrooms. The assignment that is not returned to the student for weeks loses its impetus, as does the paper that receives only a letter grade with no follow-up comments (Marzano et al., 2001).

Multiple assessment strategies make the failure to grade and hand back assignments much more avoidable. Use a variety of formal and informal assessments to communicate with your students. Distribute slips of brown paper on which students can write questions about the "muddy waters" that obscure their comprehension of the content. Pass quickly around the room having each student contribute one thing they learned in class that day. Keep records on academic and nonacademic achievement, along with portfolios of student work (including photos or videos of work that can't be documented in other ways). At every stage, involve students in the process of their own evaluation and assessment.

Instructional Strategies

Fun With Feedback

Performance-based assessment counters teacher-made multiple-choice and standardized tests by assessing students during real-world activities, or at least as close to the real world as possible. It emphasizes doing (active participation) and it usually takes places over a long period of time—from a week to even a month. The teacher and students reflect on the work, noting its strengths and weaknesses. Such feedback helps the student strengthen synaptic connections. The possible tools are unlimited:

- Advertisements
- Advice columns
- Autobiographies
- Bedtime stories
- Book jackets
- Campaign speeches
- Data sheets
- Diary entries
- Dramatic presentations

- Editorial writings
- Encyclopedia entries
- Epilogues
- Experiments
- Fairy tales
- Films
- Greeting cards
- Nutrition charts
- Paintings
- Parodies

- Petitions
- Radio programs
- Sales pitches
- Scrapbooks
- Sculptures
- Sequels
- Simulations
- Speeches
- Superstitions
- Tributes
- TV commercials

(Continued)

(Continued)

Things to Try

- Before a new lesson, give students a short questionnaire to fill out, or conduct a brief discussion to determine their background knowledge. This formative assessment will help you determine where to start the lesson (and who might need extra attention during the unit).

- Pick an important term or concept from your daily lesson and have students list ideas associated with it. For example, students in a government class might list *Native American, reservation, self-determination, rights,* and *politics* for the word *sovereignty.* Then, have students compare their lists with a partner, noting what items are common to both lists and discussing the items that appear on one list but not the other.

- Distribute empty or partially completed outlines before a class lecture or during a video, and have students fill in the blanks as information is presented. This will focus their attention and help them identify important ideas.

- Have students create a memory matrix based on categories you assign. For instance, you could compare feudalism to mercantilism with the following categories: sources of wealth, generation of wealth, distribution of wealth, and population centers. Students will see immediately what important information they remember and what they need to keep studying.

- Assign a sixty-second paper on what you covered during that day's lesson. One minute is a very small amount of class time to invest in an assignment that will tell you at a glance if students understand the main points of your lesson or are simply focusing on minor and supporting ideas.

- Have students devise a pro-and-con grid for one concept they are learning. Listing advantages and disadvantages requires them to go beyond memorizing facts to analyzing information; it reinforces their decision-making skills.

- Use concept maps—drawings that show the connections between concepts and facts—for insight into how students are thinking about their own thinking.

- Make space in your room to store student portfolios. Annotated portfolios include artifacts from class along with explanations of the significance of the selections. (Often, the relevance of the artifact is explained in terms of classroom goals and content.)

- Let students generate test questions and answers. To write a good question, they must have an understanding of the material and the key points. The quality of their questions can help you assess their weaknesses. Returning these questions to students in the form of a practice test also makes them part of the process, removing them from the role of "innocent bystander" during assessment.

Many of these ideas are from the book *Classroom Assessment Techniques: A Handbook for College Teachers (2nd Edition),* by Thomas A. Angelo and K. Patricia Cross (1998: Jossey-Bass).

ORGANIZATION ≠ OPPRESSION

The brain stores new information by identifying patterns in it. As it receives fresh material, the brain searches its established neural networks for a background against which it can comprehend the new knowledge. Anything familiar—sensory information (like a remembered scent), a pattern, a relationship—will serve as a connection to information already stored in the brain. If the brain finds nothing on which to build, it abandons the new information. Many study skills and instructional strategies are compatible with the brain's innate desire to decipher patterns. Disheartened middle and high school students make remarks about their homework like "I don't know where to start," "This stuff is so boring," and "One minute I know it, and the next I've forgotten it" because their brains have a difficult time tapping into these patterns.

Secret Revealed

 Contrary to popular belief, teens aren't looking to pick fights with the adults in their lives. They aren't arguing about skipping breakfast and borrowing the car because they enjoy the verbal sparring. Parents and teachers who give brooding teens a wide berth to avoid provoking an outburst are going at it all the wrong way. They ought to be looking for ways to guide teenagers instead.

Sound shocking? Prepare yourself for this: Teenagers actually want and need guidance from adults about important life issues like education and work plans (Schneider & Younger, 1996). This emotional support from adults is imperative to adolescents' healthy development. Don't be fooled into backing off just because of a teen's show of resistance to your advice. What may appear to be oppositional behavior is often a desire for personal autonomy. Teens want to choose their own clothes, friends, and hobbies—these things demonstrate their independence and individuality. The search for autonomy is normal; it's the beginning step toward taking on adult responsibilities. Once the argument about homework ends, however, teens are very receptive to suggestions about choosing a college or how to act during a job interview.

Help teenagers access these patterns by providing models, organization, and structure to their lives. Every student needs a planner to track assignments; it's hard to accomplish something if you're not sure what you need to do. Hold young teens accountable for keeping their planners up-to-date, and they'll maintain the habit as they grow older. Teach them how to budget their time by deciding what to study and for how long, to take advantage of mental stamina by doing the hard or boring stuff first, to establish a context for studying by always working in the same place—and nag them to get off the Internet!

It's only fair that teachers and parents help teens establish order in their lives; we are the ones who expect them to achieve academically, participate in extracurricular activities, help with many of the household chores, and perhaps hold down a job. Students have never been busier. Many adolescents barely have time to grab a snack or change clothes between activities. They hold up their part of the bargain pretty well but do better when we provide study skills and the support to perfect them.

In class, cue them. Emphasize and repeat important information. Teach students different note-taking methods (Cornell–2-column, SQ3R, outlines, or your personal favorite) and have them practice one style until they can do it automatically while listening to a lecture. Remind them to review their notes within twenty-four hours to improve their retention (and save study time in the long run). The brain remembers images more easily than words, which makes graphic organizers, pictures, charts, and graphs effective tools for organizing patterns.

My personal favorite note-taking style is Double Column notes because they allow the students to encode the information in a variety of ways and are easily modified to meet different students' needs and purposes.

Figure 3.4   Double-Column Notes

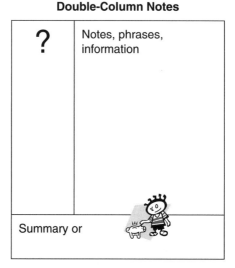

Double-Column Notes

| ? | Notes, phrases, information |

Summary or

EVERY GOOD BOY DOES FINE

While we would prefer that all learning be meaningful, in the real world people need to memorize important information that is arbitrary and dull. In classroom situations, students can benefit from mnemonics, techniques for remembering information with images and words (Carney & Levin, 2000). For example, the names of the planets or the number of days in each month are more easily memorized with the help of a mnemonic. Rhymes and acronyms are two common strategies that can be fun for students learning by rote.

A teacher may provide mnemonics, but they are more meaningful when the students construct them. Younger children do better with auditory mnemonics, such as "When two vowels go a-walking, the first one does the talking." Adolescents, with their increased mental capacities, do well with visual or auditory mnemonics like the following examples (Wang & Thomas, 1995):

- PMAT: prophase, metaphase, anaphase, telophase—the four stages of cellular mitosis.
- I Am A Person: Indian, Arctic, Atlantic, Pacific—the four oceans of the world.
- Sober Physicists Don't Find Giraffes In Kitchens: the orbital names for electrons are S, P, D, F, G, I, K.
- Associate each school supply with a particular spot in your bedroom. Imagine your backpack with your desk, band music on the bed, and PE clothes in the drawer. Before leaving for school each morning, mentally walk around the room. Have you remembered all your items? Visualizing your dresser will cue you to bring your PE clothes if you've forgotten to pack them.
- To remember that Annapolis is the capital of Maryland, visualize two apples. For St. Paul, Minnesota, imagine a saint sipping a soda.
- To remember the twelve cranial nerves (for a brain-compatible teaching class, of course), just think of the rhyme, "On Old Olympus Towering Tops, A Finn And German Viewed Some Hops": the cranial nerves are the olfactory, optic, occulomotor, trochlear, trigeminal, abducens, facial, auditory, glossopharyngeal, vagus, spinal accessory, and hypoglossal!

Time-management and test-taking strategies also should be taught to teenagers. When students have a framework for remembering information and keeping track of their due dates on calendars, they are much better prepared to cope with the cognitive and structural chaos inside their heads.

Study skills help the brain organize and make connections. Students stop cold if they are overwhelmed by too much to learn in too little time, by not knowing where to start or by not having time to let information sink in. Study strategies can make the difference between academic success and meltdown. Share the following items with your students to help them take charge of their learning.

Effective Study Strategies

- Take notes. Whether you prefer KWL (What I KNOW, What I WANT to Know, and What I LEARNED), outline, or double columns, pick one and practice it until it becomes second nature.
- Tap into prior knowledge.
- Organize information in notebooks, on note cards, or in a computer.
- Budget study time. Schedule an hour or two each day at a desk in your bedroom or school library, wherever you want. Take a ten-minute brain break every fifty minutes and stick to the plan.
- Summarize in writing what you've learned at the end of each study session.
- Monitor your learning while you study; reflect on what needs more work and what you don't understand.
- Keep an assignment notebook. Break down large assignments into smaller tasks and cross items off your list as you complete them.
- Eliminate distractions, turn off the TV, stop instant messaging, and let voicemail collect your cell phone messages.
- Be positive—as they say, "Change your thoughts, change your life."
- Do the difficult material first, while you are still fresh.

Secret Revealed

Instant messaging, googling, and downloading songs while attempting to do homework—a good thing or a bad thing? David Meyer, a psychologist who directs the Brain, Cognition, and Action Laboratory at the University of Michigan (www.umich.edu/~bcalab) warns that each interruption requires time for the brain to readjust. A small math or language arts assignment that would normally take thirty minutes, will suddenly take two or three hours if multitasking is involved.

Surprisingly, the more divergent the task, the easier the work is for the brain. If we are trying to pet our dog while we do homework, the brain continues to operate smoothly; however, if we are trying to do two similar jobs with our brain, such as instant messaging and writing a composition, the brain gets stuck on pause.

Effective Test-Taking Strategies

The pressure to perform on tests is impacting the way teachers instruct, students learn, and parents fret. Providing students with added support in the art of test taking is a requirement for the twenty-first century.

- Test prep should begin on the first day of class (and no, I'm not kidding, high schoolers)—reviews, homework, readings, and attending class, are all important parts of the process. The best way to reduce anxiety is to be prepared.
- Identify your best test-studying strategies—do you study best alone or in a group, with flash cards or highlighting, or is a combination the best?
- Eat before a test; a fully performing brain needs the energy supply food provides.
- Quickly peruse the test when you first get it and catch the general gist.
- Stay positive during the test—if you start to feel anxious, breath deeply, or use other stress-reducing tactics.
- Do the easiest problems first (this is the opposite approach of study strategies, where the most difficult assignments are tackled first).
- Be sure to complete the items with the greatest point value. If something has to give, let it be the one-pointers.
- Students, create a mock test; this requires higher-level thinking and is a good way to review.

A BETTER DAY STUDENT TEACHING

"Good morning," the student teacher said to each student as the teenagers shuffled into class. She paused now and then to ask individual students about a dance recital the night before or to compliment them on the tiebreaking goal they scored at the game. The room filled with noisy chatter as the class took their seats. She began class by passing around an empty box and asking students to put something of no real

value in it (such as pencils, pieces of paper, or movie ticket stubs). As the box went around the room, she asked the students for examples of storytelling, perhaps from their own families. When the box returned to the front of the room, she told a story about how her great-grandmother had participated in the women's suffrage movement. She punctuated elements of her tale with props from the box—the class was riveted. Afterward, the teacher divided the class and the items from the box into four groups for a cooperative learning assignment. The students told and listened to each other's stories; the signal to clean up at the end of class caught them all by surprise.

Part II

The Brain in School

4

The Literate Brain

Pamela Nevills

Scientific studies using **neuroimaging** are numerous, and educators can easily be overwhelmed with the possible implications for classroom practices. To be neurosmart without being overwhelmed is the goal of this chapter and the ones that follow. A quick review of the development of the reading decoding pathway acknowledges the value of explicit and direct teaching instruction. The education system is geared for children to learn to read; however, not as much is known about teaching students to use reading to learn. The focus of this chapter is to look at teaching strategies that will help students who know how to read to know how to approach reading for comprehension. Teaching strategies from cognitive science and classroom best practices such as the importance of connecting reading, writing, and spelling, identifying word form areas for vocabulary development, and analytical word analysis are given. Another look at the brain's way of protecting students from overload of information is uncovered as a conscious filtering system. Finally, teachers are asked to consider visualization strategies. Classroom discussions about what students picture when they read can greatly enhance the possibility that students will record, remember, and recall information at a later time. Practical classroom examples help make research relevant. Advanced reading strategies are most constructive when students have developed into natural, competent readers.

LEARNING AND GOOD READERS

Encouraging and supporting students to be successful learners is difficult to achieve in upper grades if children have not learned to read in the primary grades. Successful reading beyond the primary years can only happen if children have become automatic decoders and readers. This feat happens through adjustments to the oral language pathway. Building a decoding pathway in a child's brain is the major work of the early school years. However, if students come to school in the upper elementary or secondary school years without automatic, fluent reading skills, this deficit must be addressed and remediated.

How the Brain's Pathway for Speaking Becomes a Pathway for Reading

During the primary years, practice with **phonemes,** the smallest individual sounds in words, along with study of phonics rules, develops a few permanent detours from the oral language pathway in the brain. For most students, a revised version of the oral language pathway becomes a reading decoding pathway as they are taught through a classroom implemented reading program (Nevills & Wolfe, 2009). Other children need extended practice and review to convert an established speaking route in the brain into a reading super speedway. A small number of students need intensive intervention to force their brains to develop an automatic reading path. What is the difference between the speaking and listening oral pathway and the route used to read and identify words?

Reading Begins in the Brain's Visual Center

To speak, neurons excite a pathway from the ears through the temporal, parietal, and frontal lobes with some effort from the visual association area to bring visions of the spoken topic. Reading, however, begins with the visual center as images are received, recorded, and rerouted for identification. Once again, activation occurs in the temporal, parietal, and frontal lobes, but the initial input originates from the eyes, not the ears. A reader must be able to connect written symbols to sounds and combine sounds that form words. Once it is determined that the sounds are words, the reader wants to ascertain that the words are sensible. The words need to give meaning to others before and after them.

Angular Gyrus—Matching Letters to Sounds

The silent reading pathway that develops includes a structure, the **angular gyrus,** which has not previously been described (see Figure 4.1). This brain structure is located

Figure 4.1 The Silent Reading Pathway in the Brain

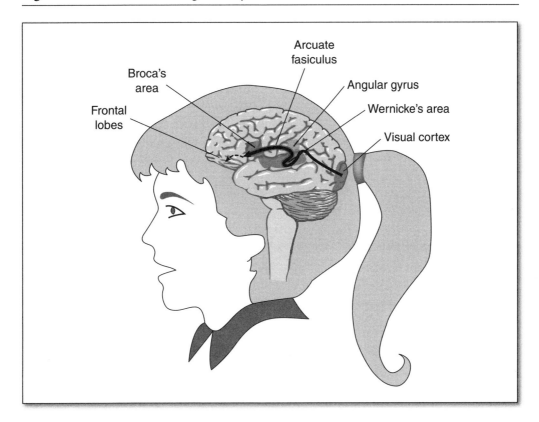

at the junction of the occipital, parietal, and temporal lobes toward the back of the cerebral cortex. This location perfectly situates the angular gyrus to be a bridge between the visual word recognition system and the rest of the language processing system (Nevills & Wolfe, 2009). Additionally, it snuggles close to Heschl's gyrus, a part of the oral pathway. As letters are interpreted in the angular gyrus, they become sounds, which we identify as the phonemes of spoken language. Realize this process begins by hearing sounds without attaching letters to them. During preschool and the early elementary years, children engage in many activities that help them play with the sounds of language. They sing songs, listen to nursery rhymes, and play games with words. "If I say *bake* and ask you to change the *b* sound to the *m* sound what word do you hear?" Or, "How many new words can you think of that end like the word *dog*?" And, "What sound do you hear in the middle of the word *swim*, and what other words do you know that have the same *I* sound in the middle?" Children engage with oral language activities, games, and whimsical playing with words during their preschool years. Then, they are generally ready for instruction that helps them to develop a pathway including and through the angular gyrus to formulate a new loop. Activation of this structure makes decoding of actual words and matching letters to sounds become an attainable task.

WHAT CAN YOU TELL YOUR STUDENTS ABOUT THE SOUNDS OF LANGUAGE?

To become a good reader, it is important to be able to hear and play with sounds. These sounds are called phonemes. Interestingly, phonemes are sounds students learn without knowing what letters make the sounds. For example, you know your brain has two hemispheres. Let's think about how the word hemisphere sounds, not how it looks with letters. Count the number of unique, individual sounds you hear when you say hemisphere. When you carefully break down the sounds into their smallest sounds, phonemes, you will most likely hear and identify eight unique sounds (h-e-m-i-s-f-e-r). And, take the word brain. Drop the B and replace it with TR. Now, you have train. Replace the ending with PS, and you have traipse, which means to prod or walk through. Using traipse, and changing the long A to short A and dropping the S ending, you have trap. Being able to do these sound manipulations in your head without seeing written letters forces your brain to build a new thinking pathway to prepare you to read. Playing with word sounds is challenging for you and necessary for the brain to understand words you read.

Spelling and Writing Ignite for Reading

The connection between spelling and writing words correctly is obvious, but the connection of spelling instruction to reading success has been less clearly defined. Authors and researchers, Malatesha Joshi, Rebecca Treiman, Suzanne Carreker, and Louisa Moats (2009) provide convincing conclusions about the importance of explicit instruction for the rules and nuances of spelling. These clinicians assert that helping children to acquire an awareness of sounds and representative letters that make up words has a direct correlation to reading comprehension. This proficiency with language is actualized through correct spelling and writing. Children take the plunge from thinking about sounds to writing letters. Accordingly, they can appropriately use words in their own writing and put meaning to words they read. These authors propose coordination of a comprehensive spelling system with any reading program (Joshi et al., 2009).

A look at spelling instruction will bring us closer to understanding how students use their brains to wrap around spelling instruction, writing, and reading as a neat productive package. To many people, spelling instruction means to memorize words and to write them repetitively until they can be retrieved from rote **nondeclarative memory.** Many poor spellers in the world today are the causalities of spelling instruction based upon the premise that spelling could best be taught by using visual memory skills through drill and repetition.

The English language is predictable enough for comprehensive spelling instruction. Only a very small percentage of words cannot be taught by sound-symbol relationship, understanding the origin of the word (Anglo-Saxon, Greek, or Latin), or identification of single sounds in words that do not follow orthographic rules. This small amount, about 4% of English words needs to be taught through the brain's visual memory system. Repetitive learning activities hold words lacking conventional spelling in working memory until they are remembered by rote recall. The remaining majority of words in the English language, however, can be taught sequentially and in tandem with words introduced for decoding in reading instruction.

A proposed educational sequence to combine instruction for decoding words and spelling begins in kindergarten (see Table 4.1). During the first year of school, children learn letters that make only one phonemic sound while they also learn names for the corresponding letters. They begin also to memorize sight vocabulary. First-grade students learn regular consonant and vowel sounds and their letter correspondences. They learn common patterns for sounds that allow them to read fully decodable text selections. A few exceptions to rules for phonics are also learned. By second grade, students are ready for more complex letter patterns and common patterns for word endings. Multisyllabic words, unstressed vowels, and common prefixes and suffixes are learned in third grade. Students in the fourth grade learn Latin-based prefixes, suffixes, and roots. Greek combining forms can be introduced during fifth through seventh grade (Joshi et al., 2009). As a child's brain builds upon the spoken language pathway, developing a spelling system to express language through writing is a critical attribute to the **reading system** that develops and expands simultaneously.

Table 4.1 An Educational Sequence for Combined Word Decoding and Spelling Programs

Kindergarten: Phonetic sounds produced by one letter and the corresponding letter name and some sight vocabulary

First Grade: Consonant and vowel sounds and the letters that make them, more decodable words, some exceptions, and an expanded sight vocabulary

Second Grade: More complex letter patterns and common patterns for word endings are identified and applied to spelling and writing

Third Grade: Multisyllabic words, unstressed vowels, and common prefixes and suffixes are found in reading and spelling instruction

Fourth Grade: Latin-based prefixes, suffixes, and roots add to a growing vocabulary for reading, writing, listening, and speaking

Fifth Through Eighth Grade: Words based upon the Greek language and other words found in content level texts and reading selections (Joshi, Treiman, Carreker, & Moats, 2009)

WHAT CAN YOU TELL YOUR STUDENTS ABOUT THE IMPORTANCE OF WRITING AND SPELLING?

Words are funny. They can be spoken, listened to, read, and written. In the brain, there are a series of pathways connecting different senses and thinking systems for the purpose of transporting words. It is quite like an interchange in a very large city. Cars, like neurons, move in every direction coming from various locations as their drivers are determined to arrive at a variety of locations. So it is with words in the brain. Reading starts with the eyes seeing letters representing words. Speaking begins with a thought or vision to be described from a memory system and is produced through the motor cortex as understandable sounds. Writing is initiated much like speaking but is carried out through motor control of the hands as they direct a writing instrument. Listening originates in the ears and records in a memory system. No one else knows what you hear, unless you write or repeat it. Think about this flurry of activity all around words and how it helps us to understand why we use four different types of vocabulary: reading, speaking, writing, and listening. They are all interrelated and important to us as learners. Think and talk about which types of vocabulary might be readily accessed and have a larger volume. Can you read and understand a larger variety of complex words than you are able to use in conversation? Why do you think that happens?

[Students are directed to realize that we have a much larger reading and writing vocabulary than what we are able to use when speaking. This happens because during reading and writing the brain is in an automatic-pilot mode. It is able to access an extensive vocabulary that is stored in long term memory. When we speak, we can access words that are not only known but also must be available to be pronounced. The very act of speaking and interpreting feedback from the listener or audience limits the brain's capacity to find more advanced words.]

The Brain's Silent Reading (Decoding) Pathway

A blending of reading instruction, including deep understanding of how words are identified for their sounds, letters, and spelling sequence, reinforces and reconfigures the oral language pathway to form a silent reading pathway (see Figure 4.2). If you attempt to identify when you became a reader, most likely it will be difficult for you to think of a day or even an approximate age that you could celebrate as your *day or age of reading independence*. At some point during your elementary years, you just knew you could pick up a book and read without someone else's help. Brain development that allows a person to read is nothing less than spectacular. Neuroscience tells us that when the **myelination** of the axons in specific systems occurs, the system is able to operate with efficiency. The reading decoding pathway becomes mature when glial cells on the axons of the pathway are developed. The system is said to be myelinated

Figure 4.2 Flow Chart of the Silent Reading Pathway

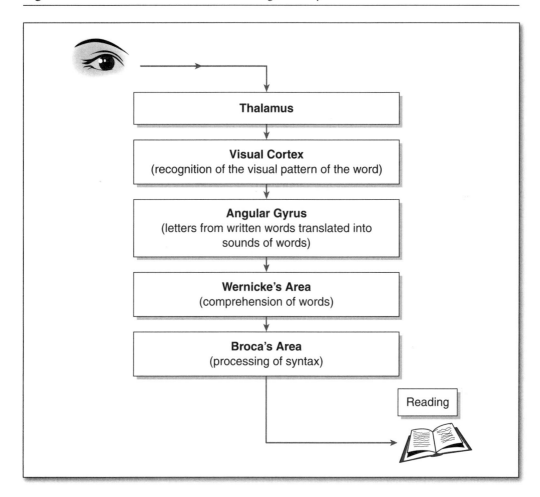

and the process of building for reading is complete. When the reading decoding pathway has axons that are coated with glial cells, reading becomes automatic. The dividend of spending time practicing reading out loud and silently, drilling the rules of orthographic language through a phonics and spelling program, applying rules and exceptions to words and phrases, and rehearsing sight vocabulary through visual memory comes to fruition. The system is fully operational, and the elementary aged child no longer needs to focus on learning to read; the reading system is ready (though still needing to be advanced and tweaked) to be used to learn.

COMPREHENSIBLE READING

Educators in the primary grades know the "science" of teaching reading. During the last 10 to 15 years, textbook publishers and educators have diligently reviewed research, learned new programs and approaches to teaching, and have persistently applied new reading procedures to their teaching toolkits. Neuroscience is now rapidly validating successful outcomes from systematic instruction by producing brain scans of reading structures from students who have undergone clinical reading remediation. There is evidence of increased myelination in the word identification areas of the brain. This increase means the area is developed and accessed during word identification tasks (Keller & Just, 2009). Scientific teaching with direct, systematic instruction can potentially permeate every necessary skill students need to become accurate, rapid word decoders. Students practice lists of sight words and commit them to memory. Simultaneously, readers build skills for lower level comprehension as they answer questions of *who, what, when, where,* and *why.* This portion of reading instruction and skill attainment is known and in place in most, if not all, schools. Basically, we know how students learn to read, and when they do not succeed we know what to do to help them overcome their struggles.

These bold statements could not have been written in the early 1990s. But since then, the country is focused on being a nation of readers. Word calling and word decoding are not the end of the story for reading teachers. Advanced instructional techniques are necessary for upper elementary and secondary school students. Moving beyond initial skill development, teachers find students' curious brains and advanced learning capabilities demand more stringent instruction. Reading becomes increasingly complex for older students.

Beyond Building a Reading Brain

Teaching children to read is the most studied process in the reading and language arts process, and it is the easiest to teach. It can be quite a prescriptive although detailed process. The more brain challenging task of reading to learn and understand content for upper elementary grades and into high school is multidimensional, but it is underacknowledged by research and instructional planners. Students must grow extensive word networks for complex vocabulary, develop deep comprehension for words in increasingly long sentences, and become empowered with neuron connections to various areas of the brain to be able to answer questions that involve analysis and synthesis. How can reading with this level of intensity be taught?

Reading with automaticity, fluency, and understanding is developed during the upper elementary grades. A series of higher order thinking skills necessary for expert reading constitutes an impressive list.

Advanced vocabulary development

Rapid thought processing

Deep understanding of phrases and collective sentences

Familiarity of word conventions and networks

Evaluation and analysis of published works

Organized thinking and problem solving

Synthesis of thoughts for writing and speaking

Development of research reports accessing a variety of resources

Communication of thoughts and concepts stimulated by reading

Utilization of technology as an information and communication system

The reading curriculum must utilize the benefits technology can bring to encourage the type of brain power needed for these reading abilities. Fortunately, neurologists with educators as their partners are beginning to see this as a viable area for study.

Development of Word Form Areas

For students to develop advanced reading skills, we look again at how their brains have organized themselves, quite unconsciously, for reading. Sally Shaywitz (2003) reports that word form systems are used to analyze words for their model (word form), spelling, pronunciation, and meaning. The occipital and temporal lobe junction is the site of storage for these **ganglion,** which constitute congregations of related neurons. A word envisioned sets off a string of neural activation about that word and all the information stored to relate to the word. During silent reading, a skilled reader can speed through text fully engaging, exciting, and igniting chemical and electrical reactions among word form areas as one word is identified and another added to create meaningful interpretations. The most successful readers are identified not only by their word calling ability but also by the unconscious act of creating stormlike activity in the word form areas in the occipital and temporal regions of the brain.

Teachers help students establish extensive word form areas during instruction and reflective conversation. Yes, it is still important to learn and study vocabulary in Grades 4 through 12. Janet Allen (2009), teacher and author, during a presentation at the Illinois Reading Council Conference, provided the following technique to build connections among word networks. Word networks are commonly known by educators as *background information.* The teacher selects critical words, proper nouns, and meaningful phrases from the reading passage. Fifteen to 20 items are appropriate. Students are asked to work with a partner and to write a sentence for each of the words or phrases. Each sentence cannot have more than two of the vocabulary terms. Next, a classroom set of sentences is generated and recorded for all to see. The sentences are recorded as they are given by students, and they are not changed if vocabulary is incorrectly used. Note, the incorrect predictions are not copied by the students or rehearsed, they are just listed. It is not recommended educational or cognitive practice to have students focus and attend to erroneous thinking that requires replacement learning.

Each day when the students finish reading, they go back to the sentences to determine if they are true or false based on what they read. After the students have read about one-third of the selection, or three chapters of a book, they return to the sentences as a class. Students rearrange the words or revise the sentences to reflect what has been read. This type of rich, interactive vocabulary experience allows students to interact among peers, build background information, and fortify word networks for future recall. This teaching strategy can be used with any content area, according to Allen. In a biology class, the words selected for study could be the teacher's choice, the textbook author's predetermined list, or the words in the textbook printed in bold (Allen, 2009).

WHAT CAN YOU TELL YOUR STUDENTS ABOUT THE COMPLEXITIES OF READING?

Knowing how to pronounce and define words is work for the early years of school. Schoolwork becomes increasingly complex, and the number of pages students are expected to read become large as students advance through the grades. Sometimes, college students are expected to read hundreds of pages between the time their class meets on Monday and the next class meeting on Wednesday. How do students in the middle school and high school years prepare to become ferocious readers ready to take on the demands of advanced schooling or, as adults, jobs that demand they are familiar with technical journals or company procedures? To be able to read heavy volumes of printed materials requires lots and lots of reading of many different types of reading materials. While you build vocabulary for reading, word form clusters build in your brain. Soon, you are able to identify words and their multiple meanings depending upon the contents of the passage you are reading.

You would know from a previous example that the word hemispheres *is referring to our planet earth and not to your brain in this sentence. The northern and southern hemispheres are divided by an imaginary line called the* equator. *As you read, your neurons are igniting in various areas of your brain. The temporal lobes are identifying the sounds. Feelings you have about the words are exciting the parietal lobes. Visual pictures of the words are being created in the occipital lobes. During the nanosecond that all of this action is happening, the frontal lobes are putting it all together to help you understand what you are reading. As pathways cross and connect throughout your brain, you identify what the words mean and how much of what you read you will remember. It is not simple to explain, but your brain does all these things instantaneously, automatically, and unconsciously when you are a skilled, fluent reader.*

Analytical and Anchored Word Analysis

Reading with a fluent, sophisticated activation pattern differs from initial reading that relies on the silent or oral reading decoding pathway. The reading decoding pathway is activated by advanced readers only when a word is unknown and needs to be analyzed. Research by Juel and Deffes (2004) tells about successful word identification techniques for advanced readers. Contrary to reading practices used in many classrooms today, research does not support word identification through *contextual clues.* This strategy relies solely on reader background and experience. It does not strengthen the possibility that the word will be recognized when it is encountered again. Interestingly, research by these two specialists supports what we know about how the reading brain works.

A student can be directed to **analyze** a word by seeking the distinguishing characteristics of the word and to involve the senses. Determining how the word looks, sounds, feels, and applies to the reader's unique interests allows the word to be held in an association loop in working memory. This intense analysis increases the likelihood the student will remember the word the next time it appears in oral or written language. The process also fortifies possibilities that the word will move into long term memory storage with other similar words.

A second approach supported by the same research is the **anchored** condition. This strategy also exemplifies how the brain is most effective by focusing on properties of the word, its beginning, ending, root, and sounds. The student looks closely at the word to search for other words with the same or different meanings (Juel & Duffes, 2004). For example, in the following sentence, *The distinguished scientist tripped on his way to the platform where he was to receive an award,* the word *distinguished* is very similar to *disgruntled, disgusted, disturbed,* or *distraught.* Looking specifically at the beginning and ending of the word could lead to an incorrect choice, but including the middle of the word separates it from the rest of the choices. Combining an analytical and anchored approach, students could be asked to think of other words that have the same or similar meanings. Identifying the words *respected, honorable,* and *admired,* for example helps to cement the word in the word form area for the next time it appears. An anchored or analytical approach to word analysis for expert readers increases the opportunity for words to be moved to the semantic, declarative memory system and to be remembered.

SERIOUS BRAIN MATTERS—MORE ABOUT THE BRAIN'S FILTERING SYSTEMS

The previous chapter explained that unnecessary sensory stimuli—a cough, a plane flying overhead, the hum of the air-conditioning motor, or numerous other distractions—are simply dropped from memory as if they never happened. Inhibitory neurons exist in the thalamus, the brain's central control center for incoming data. These special neurons offer protection. The brain does not have to think about every input from the sensory system. Most are no more than annoying disruptions to what is important in the environment. The system our brains use for protection from overload is even more complex, as neuroscience has identified another inhibitory system.

Filtering Unnecessary Information

Researchers uncovered evidence that the basal ganglia, an area involved with important movement and other tasks, and the prefrontal cortex, the rational, thinking, problem-solving part of the brain, are particularly active during filtering trials. Cognitive specialists identify the basal ganglia's function. The basal ganglia are described as a group of subcortical nuclei located under the motor cortex and are involved with modulating the frontal cortex (Nolte, 2002). They regulate and inhibit automatic movement (Carter, 1998; Sylwester, 2005). Nolte provides a broader sweep at the multivariate role of the basal ganglia and the strategic structures included in its area of the brain:

> Although the precise function of most of these connections is unknown, there has been enough recent progress that we can not only consider the consequences of damage to some of these connections, but also begin to speculate about their normal function. (Nolte, 2002, p. 469)

The connections referred to by Nolte (2002) are multiple circuits or loops among the structures of the frontal lobes, parietal and temporal lobes, as well as most other cortical areas, the somatosensory and motor cortices, the thalamus, and the basal ganglia. These loops are possible as neurotransmitters excite or inhibit the connections between neurons. The conclusion is that the basal ganglia, in addition to its known role of influencing motor activities, has been identified as active during the very act of strengthening connections for learning or inhibiting actions to interrupt or weaken the strength of action.

Research Support for This Second Filtering System

In 2004, Russell Poldrack and Paul Rodriguez from the University of California, Los Angeles, were interested in classification learning. By using functional neuroimaging, they looked for interactions between the basal ganglia and the medial temporal lobes. They were particularly interested in how medial temporal lobe activation and deactivation happens during learning. They attempted to link learner attention and engagement with the brain's memory systems. Their work suggests that different memory systems compete for the brain's attention based upon the demands of the task and the behavioral success experienced by the learner. These researchers found the **prefrontal lobes,** interacting with the basal ganglia, to be moderators of which competing memory system would be energized. Filtering or interference created by these brain structures formed negative signals to modulate activity in the hippocampus, which is known for its important role in holding and manipulating the brain's working or short term memories.

Studies from Poldrack and Rodriguez (2004) are far from conclusive about the complex interactive nature of the brain's structures during learning. McCollough and Vogel (2008), from the Department of Psychology at the University of Oregon, are also attuned to learning and learner responsiveness. They analyzed and reported on research conducted by McNab and Kingberg. The selected study looked at visual working memory and attention of participants. McNab and Kingberg required study subjects to consciously select visual stimuli for their focus. Participants were asked to select objects of certain colors and to ignore other colors. Predisposed concentration required an inhibitory brain system, which is different from the unconscious filtering of unneeded information by the thalamus.

Imaging techniques used by the neuroscientists showed an additional system. There was increased activity in the prefrontal cortex, including the area of the basal ganglia. The structures of the basal ganglia were identified as they acted with the prefrontal cortex to excite or inhibit information. The task described required study subjects to control the flow of information into working memory. Rather than being limited to controlling movements of the human body, the newly identified actions of the basal ganglia affect *conscious decisions needed for learning.* This recent study adds to our understanding of the brain's ability to limit incoming stimulus and to allow a student select what is important to learn.

Classroom Implications

Implications from this study are exciting for educators. Outcomes from studies by neuroscientists are beginning to show educators how students are cognitively equipped to select and become engaged with content educators present during lessons. For successful learning, students must want to learn. Figure 4.3 shows the brain as it halts unneeded information first at the thalamus then at the basal ganglia and prefrontal cortex. The basal ganglia system acts as a police system to protect the brain by allowing the learner to make conscious decisions that stop unnecessary

Figure 4.3   Diagram of the Brain's Systems for Filtering Information With the Thalamus (Unconscious) and Basal Ganglia Systems

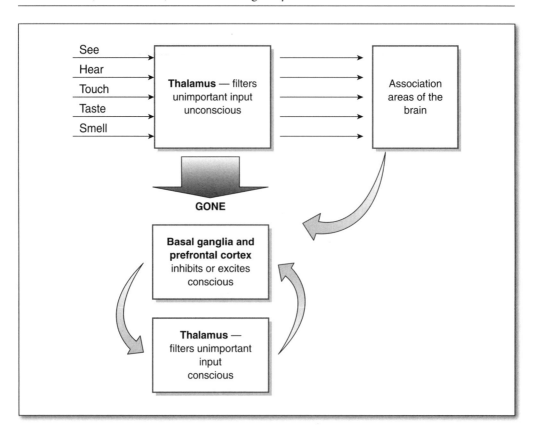

noise or distracting input data. Notice that information selected to be worthy of more consideration flows through connecting fibers back to the thalamus. From there, it is distributed for interpretation in the association areas of the brain. Working memory is dependent upon a constant rehearsal of information and a loop that continues to associate new information with what is already known.

Students consciously select what is worthy of their concentrated efforts. Teachers cannot make students decide to engage with information from their lessons, but they can make the learning environment appeal to the curious and personal nature of the human brain. Giving students information about how their brains respond to new information and helping students to gage how much time they personally need for rehearsal and revisiting is inherently an effective teaching strategy. Students need to be aware that it is an individual choice to practice and study. Information students select to learn ultimately is transferred into long term memory for recording, remembering, and recalling.

WHAT CAN YOU TELL YOUR STUDENTS ABOUT THE CHOICES THEY MAKE FOR LEARNING?

Earlier, we talked about how you can own and control information to cement it into long term memory. The steps you take are represented by words beginning with the letter R. They are recognizing, reducing, recording, remembering, *and* recalling. *Tell your partner how these steps happen by talking about how your brain works to access long term memory.*

Now, we will add a new piece of information. You realize that most of the input you receive from your senses is not acknowledged by your memory systems. Most information is forgotten, and you do not have to even think about it. There is another system that filters information and allows you to decide if you want to think about it enough to remember it. This area of your brain is in the prefrontal lobes at the forehead area of your brain. It joins with small structures called the basal ganglia. *The basal ganglion system was identified by neuroscience as controlling unconscious physical movement. New research studies show that the basal ganglia also allows you to decide if you are interested enough to rehearse and try to remember something you have received from your senses. For example, let's say your study in science has to do with genetics, the study of biological processes to transmit unique characteristics of a living organism to its offspring. You have a choice. You can jump into the study by thinking about how this information can be exciting and important for you to know. Or, you can think it is boring and decide to expend as little cognitive energy as possible to just get by during the study. If you choose to engage with the information, you will practice and manipulate it through a series of steps as you recognize, reduce, record, remember, and recall information that has meaning and is interesting to you. If you choose to slack off with this topic, chances are you will not make a good grade, nor will you remember the slightest bit of information when you need it later in your school years or in your adult life.*

Visualizing Words and Comprehending Meaning

Students need to understand what they read, but the task is not a simple one. This critical aspect of competent reading requires activation of the occipital lobes and the brain's visual system. Again, neuroscience provides insight into what is happening in the brain. Interestingly, the visual system is critical to young children as their sight matures. Young children see objects, tag a name on the object, and learn to pronounce the word. The visual association system allows children to learn to speak. When children learn to read, the visual system is challenged to adapt to receive and interpret arbitrary shapes in the form of letters and combinations of letters. The input in symbols needs to be matched to images stored in long term memory to comprehend what is conveyed on a page of written letters and words. The reading process starts with the oral language pathway, which developed from pictures provided by the occipital lobes. Reading switches the direction as the proficient reader turns words back to the visual association center of the brain to interpret in pictures what is being read. It is not quite that simple, as sometimes what is being read not only creates pictures or images but also emotions and feelings. It is easily seen that comprehension requires much more of the brain's physical structures and capacity and is a much more advanced reading action than merely identifying words through the reading decoding pathway.

Teaching strategies to take advantage of the visual aspects of comprehension were identified by Nanci Bell as early as 1986. Her teaching tool, *Visualizing and Verbalizing for Language Comprehension and Thinking* (Bell, 1991), created a flurry of interest in the education field. Not much was known about the reading brain and its complex pathway. Now, it is more common knowledge that the brain initially uses the visual system to learn words and then reverses the system to understand the words it read. Bell's teaching techniques helped children who read well, but it could not answer comprehension questions. The author and researcher discovered a direct relationship between making visual images, comprehending text, and thinking about what was read. Readers can be encouraged to make pictures when they read. Students are asked to imagine and describe what they read. Vocabulary selected to describe what a child envisioned reveals that all students conjure similar, but not identical, images from the same passage. Connoisseurs of neuroscience know that different images are created by each student due to personal unique memories stored in long term memory systems. Activated word form clusters allow individually invented pictures of thought. Here are examples of prompts to stimulate visualizing and picture forming.

Think about how the people looked. Describe the characteristics of the people in this region of the world.

Picture the mama grizzly and her cub. What words would you use to tell inherent characteristics between these two animals?

Picture the historical figure you read about, and think of how you would describe him or her to your reading group.

Make a mind image of William. Choose some words that tell how William felt when he was discovered hiding the money.

What does the word *majestic* mean in this sentence? Describe a scene you remember that was majestic.

There are no right or wrong answers to these prompts. Rich conversation is likely to result. Deeper thinking is required as students are requested to infer, deduce, or predict based upon visual images they create in their minds after reading a section or passage.

Neurosmart Strategies—What Is Next?

Neuroscience helps educators and parents understand older students as they view themselves. As they mature, teens learn they can be competent yet unpredictable learners. Teachers of secondary schools can look at adult learning preferences to find that they closely align with high school students' learning preferences. Yet, classrooms may be more closely associated with learning practices that appeal to younger children. Preteen and teen years are laden with developmental and neurological changes. The next chapter answers questions about brain maturation and poses a new question about developing young adults: Is unacceptable adolescent behavior a result of brain underdevelopment, or could environmental issues have an equal or greater impact on teen behavior?

Chapter 5

The Numerate Brain

David A. Sousa

> *Mathematics possesses not only truth,*
> *but some supreme beauty—a beauty*
> *cold and austere, like that of sculpture.*
>
> —Bertrand Russell

Counting up to small quantities comes naturally to children. Either spontaneously or by imitating their peers, they begin to solve simple arithmetic problems based on counting, with or without words. Their first excursion into calculation occurs when they add two sets by counting them both on their fingers. Gradually they learn to add without using their fingers and, by the age of five, demonstrate an understanding of commutativity of addition (the rule that a + b is always equal to b + a). But as calculations become more difficult, errors abound, even for adults. One thing is certain: The human brain has serious problems with calculations. Nothing in its evolution prepared it for the task of memorizing dozens of multiplication facts or for carrying out the multistep operations required for two-digit subtraction. Our

> *Our ability to approximate numerical quantities may be embedded in our genes, but dealing with exact symbolic calculation can be an error-prone ordeal.*

ability to approximate numerical quantities may be embedded in our genes, but dealing with exact symbolic calculation can be an error-prone ordeal.

DEVELOPMENT OF CONCEPTUAL STRUCTURES

Conceptual structures about numbers develop early and allow children to experiment with calculations in their preschool years. They quickly master many addition and subtraction strategies, carefully selecting those that are best suited to a particular problem. As they apply their algorithms, they mentally determine how much time it took them to make the calculation and the likelihood that the result is correct. Siegler (1989) studied children using these strategies, and he concluded that they compile detailed statistics on their success rate with each algorithm. Gradually, they revise their collection of strategies and retain those that are most appropriate for each numerical problem.

Here is a simple example. Ask a young boy to solve 9 − 3. You may hear him say, "nine . . . eight is one . . . seven is two . . . six is three . . . six!" In this instance, he counts backward starting from the larger number. Now ask him to calculate 9 − 6. Chances are that rather than counting backward as he did in the first problem, he will find a more efficient solution. He counts the number of steps it takes to go from the smaller number to the larger: "six . . . seven is one . . . eight is two . . . nine is three . . . three!" But how did the child know this? With practice, the child recognizes that if the number to be subtracted is not very close in value to the starting number, then it is more efficient to count backward from the larger number. Conversely, if the number to be subtracted is close in value to the starting number, then it is faster to count up from the smaller number. By spontaneously discovering and applying this strategy, the child realizes that it takes him the same number of steps, namely three, to calculate 9 − 3 and 9 − 6.

Exposure at home to activities involving arithmetic no doubt plays an important role in this process by offering children new algorithms and by providing them with a variety of rules for choosing the best strategy. In any case, the dynamic process of creating, refining, and selecting algorithms for basic arithmetic is established in most children before they reach kindergarten.

> *The dynamic process of creating, refining, and selecting algorithms for basic arithmetic is established in most children before they reach kindergarten.*

Exactly how number structures develop in young children is not completely understood. However, in recent years, research in cognitive neuroscience has yielded sufficient clues about brain development to the point that researchers have devised a timeline of how number structures evolve in the brain in the early years. Sharon Griffin

(2002) and her colleagues reviewed the research and developed tests that assessed large groups of children between the ages of 3 and 11 in their knowledge of numbers, units of time, and money denominations. As a result of the students' performance on these tests, they made some generalizations about the development of conceptual structures related to numbers in children within this age range. Their work is centered on several core assumptions about how the development of conceptual structures progresses. Three assumptions of particular relevance are as follows:

1. Major reorganization in children's thinking occurs around the age of five when cognitive structures that were created in earlier years are integrated into a hierarchy.

2. Important changes in cognitive structures occur about every two years during the development period. The ages of 4, 6, 8, and 10 are used in this model because they represent the midpoint of the development phases (ages 3 to 5, 5 to 7, 7 to 9, and 9 to 11).

3. This developmental progression is typical for about 60 percent of children in a modern, developed culture. Thus, about 20 percent of children will develop at a faster rate while about 20 percent will progress at a slower rate.

Structures in Four-Year-Olds

The innate capabilities of young children to subitize and do some simple finger counting enables them by the age of four to create two conceptual structures, one for global quantity differences and one for the initial counting of objects (Figure 5.1). Looking for global quantity, they can tell which of two stacks of chips is more or less, which of two time units is shorter or longer, and which of two monetary units is worth more or less. On a balance scale, they can tell which side is heavier and/or lighter and which side of the beam will go down. Children at this age are still relying more on subitizing than counting, but they do know that a set of objects will get bigger if one or more objects are added or smaller if one or more objects are removed.

Counting skills are also developing. They know that each number word occurs in a fixed sequence and that each number word can be assigned to only one object in a collection.

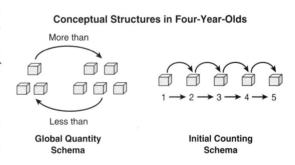

Conceptual Structures in Four-Year-Olds

More than

Less than

Global Quantity Schema

1 → 2 → 3 → 4 → 5

Initial Counting Schema

Figure 5.1   At the age of four, children have developed two major structures: one for global quantity that relies on subitizing and one for counting a small number of objects, mainly through one-to-one correspondence with fingers. (Adapted with permission from Griffin, 2002)

They also know that the last number word said indicates the size of the collection. Most can count to five, and some can count to 10. Yet, despite these counting capabilities, these children still rely more on subitizing to make quantity determinations. This may be because the global quantity structure is stored in a different part of the brain from the counting structure and because these two regions have not yet made strong neural connections with each other.

Structures in Six-Year-Olds

Children around six years of age have integrated their global quantity and initial counting models into a larger structure representing the mental number line we discussed in Chapter 1. Because this advancement gives children a major tool for making sense of quantities in the real world, it is referred to as the central conceptual structure for whole numbers. Using this higher-order structure, children recognize that numbers higher up in the counting sequence indicate quantities that are larger than numbers lower down (Figure 5.2). Moreover, they realize that numbers themselves have magnitude, that is, that 7 is bigger than 5. The number line also allows them to do simple addition and subtraction without an actual set of objects just by counting forward or backward along the line. This developmental stage is a major turning point because children come to understand that mathematics is not just something that occurs out in the environment but can also occur inside their own heads.

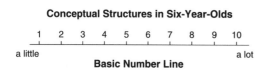

Figure 5.2 At the age of six years, children have developed a mental number line that gives them a central conceptual structure for whole numbers. (Adapted with permission from Griffin, 2002)

Now children begin using their counting skills in a broad range of new contexts. They realize that counting numbers can help them read the hour hand on a clock, determine which identical-sized money bill is worth the most, and know that a dime is worth more than a nickel even though it is smaller in size. Unlike four-year-olds, they rely more now on counting than global quantity in determining the number of objects, such as chips in a stack and weights on a balance.

Structures in Eight-Year-Olds

Children at the age of eight have differentiated their complex conceptual structure into a double mental counting line schema that allows them to represent two quantitative variables in a loosely coordinated fashion. Now they understand place value and can mentally solve double-digit addition problems and know which of two double-digit numbers is smaller or larger. The double number line structure also permits them to read the hours and minutes on a clock, to solve money problems that involve two monetary dimensions such as dollars and cents, and to solve balance-beam problems in which distance from the fulcrum as well as number of weights must be computed.

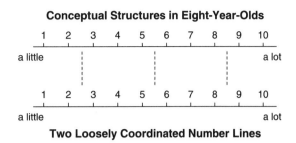

Figure 5.3   By the age of eight, children can manipulate numbers along two number lines that are loosely coordinated. (Adapted with permission from Griffin, 2002)

Structures in Ten-Year-Olds

By the age of 10, children have expanded the double number line structure to handle two quantities in a well-coordinated fashion or to include a third quantitative variable. They now acquire a deeper understanding of the whole number system. Thus, they can perform mental computations with double-digit numbers that involve borrowing and carrying, and can solve problems involving triple-digit numbers. In effect, they can make compensations along one quantitative variable to allow for changes along the other variable. This new structure also allows them to translate from hours to minutes and determine which of two times, say three hours or 150 minutes, is longer. They find it easy to translate from one monetary dimension to another, such as from quarters to nickels and dimes, to determine who has more money, and also to solve balance-beam problems where the distance from the fulcrum and number of weights both vary.

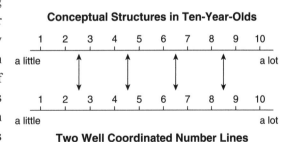

Figure 5.4   By the age of 10, children can manipulate numbers along two mental number lines that are well coordinated and thus can perform mental computations with double-digit numbers. (Adapted with permission from Griffin, 2002)

DEALING WITH MULTIPLICATION

Up to this point, we have been exploring how young children manipulate numbers using simple addition and subtraction. In school, they eventually encounter a process called multiplication, sometimes described by teachers as successive addition. However, the mental processes required to perform multiplication are more involved and somewhat different from the innate processes used for addition and subtraction. Imaging studies show that the brain recruits more neural networks during multiplication than during subtraction (Ischebeck et al., 2006). This should come as no surprise because addition and subtraction were sufficiently adequate to allow our ancestors to survive. As a result, humans need to devise learning tools to help them conquer multiplication.

Why Are Multiplication Tables Difficult to Learn?

Do you remember your first encounters with the multiplication tables as a primary student? Did you have an easy or difficult time memorizing them? How well do you know them today? Despite years of practice, most people have great difficulty with the multiplication tables. Ordinary adults of average intelligence make mistakes about 10 percent of the time. Even some of the single-digit multiplications, such as 8×7 and 9×7, can take up to two seconds, and have an error rate of 25 percent (Devlin, 2000). Why do we have such difficulty? Several factors contribute to our troubles with numbers. They include associative memory, pattern recognition, and language. Oddly enough, these are three of the most powerful and useful features of the human brain.

Multiplication and Memory

Until the late 1970s, psychologists thought that simple addition and multiplication problems were solved by a counting process carried out primarily by working memory. In 1978, Ashcraft (1995) and his colleagues began a series of experiments to test this notion with young adults. He found that most adults take about the same time to add or multiply two digits. However, it took increasingly longer to do these calculations as the digits got larger, even though the time remained the same for adding or multiplying. It took less than a second to determine the results of $2 + 3$ or 2×3, but about 1.3 seconds to solve $8 + 7$ or 8×7. If multiplication is being processed in working memory, shouldn't it take longer to multiply two digits than to add them, seeing that more counting is involved? After many experiments, Ashcraft proposed the only reasonable conclusion that was consistent with the experimental data: Solutions to the calculation problems were being retrieved from a memorized table stored in long-term memory. No counting or processing was occurring in working memory.

This effect is not that surprising for three reasons. First, we already noted in Chapter 1 that the accuracy of our mental representation of numerosity drops quickly with increasing number size. Second, the order in which we acquired arithmetic skills plays a role, because we tend to remember best that which comes first in a learning episode. When we began learning our arithmetic facts, we started with simple problems containing small digits, and the difficult problems with large digits came later. Third, because smaller digits appear more frequently in problems than larger ones, we most likely received much less practice with multiplication problems involving larger numbers.

Now, you may be saying: "So what's the big deal? We are using what we memorized in the early grades to solve arithmetic problems today. Isn't that normal?" It may be normal, but it is not natural. Preschool children use their innate but limited notions of numerosity to develop intuitive counting strategies that will help them understand and measure larger quantities. But they never get to continue following this intuitive process. When these children enter the primary grades, they encounter a sudden shift from their intuitive understanding of numerical quantities and counting strategies to the rote learning of arithmetic. Suddenly, progressing with calculations now means acquiring and storing in memory a large database of numerical knowledge, which may or may not have meaning. They also discover that some of the words they use in conversation take on different meanings when doing arithmetic. Many children persevere with this major upheaval in their mental arithmetic and language systems despite the difficulties. Unfortunately, most children also lose their intuition about arithmetic in the process.

> *Children in the primary grades encounter a sudden shift from their intuitive understanding of numerical quantities and counting strategies to the rote learning of arithmetic facts. Unfortunately, most children lose their intuition about arithmetic in the process.*

Is the Way We Teach the Multiplication Tables Intuitive?

Not really. Through hours of practice, young children expend enormous amounts of neural energy laboring over memorizing the multiplication tables, encountering high rates of error and frustration. Yet this is happening at a same time when they can effortlessly acquire the pronunciation, meaning, and spelling of 10 new vocabulary words every day. They certainly do not have to recite their vocabulary words and their meanings over and over the way they do their multiplication tables. Furthermore, they remember the names of their friends, addresses, phone numbers, and book titles with hardly any trouble. Obviously, nothing is wrong with their memories, except when it comes to the multiplication tables. Why are they so difficult for children and adults to remember?

One answer is that the way we most often teach the multiplication tables is counterintuitive. Usually, we start with the one times table and work our way up to the ten times table. Taught step-by-step in this fashion results in 100 (10 × 10) separate facts to be memorized. But is this really the best way to teach them? Children have little difficulty remembering the one and ten times tables because they are consistent with their intuitive numbering scheme and base-10 finger manipulation strategy. Now that leaves 64 separate facts (each one of 2, 3, 4, 5, 6, 7, 8, 9, multiplied by each of 2, 3, 4, 5, 6, 7, 8, 9). But why memorize all 64 separate facts? We noted at the beginning of this chapter that children already recognize the commutativity of addition by age five. By simply showing them commutativity in multiplication (3 × 8 is the same as 8 × 3), we can cut the total number of 64 separate facts nearly in half, to just 36 (The number of four pairs of identical numbers, e.g., 2 × 2 or 5 × 5, cannot be reduced) . This is a more manageable number, but it still does not solve the problem.

Some critics say that students are just not putting in the effort to memorize their multiplication facts. Others wonder whether this endeavor is even necessary, given the prevalence of electronic calculators. But these ideas beg the question: Why do our ordinarily good memories have such difficulty with this task? There is something to be learned here about the nature of memory and the structure of the multiplication tables.

Patterns and Associations

The human brain is a five-star pattern recognizer. Human memory recall often works by association, that is, one thought triggers another in long-term memory. Someone mentions mother, and the associative areas in your brain's temporal lobes generate an image in your mind's eye. Long-term storage sites are activated, and you recall the first time she took you to the zoo. The limbic region in the brain sprinkles your memory with emotions. You were so excited then because you didn't realize that elephants were so wide or giraffes so tall. More connections are made, and you fondly remember the same excitement in your own children on their first zoo visit. The brain's ability to detect patterns and make associations is one of its greatest strengths, and is often referred to as associative memory. In fact, humans can recognize individuals without even looking at their faces. Through associative

> *Associative memory is a powerful and useful capability. Unfortunately, associative memory runs into problems in areas like the multiplication tables, where various pieces of information must be kept from interfering with each other.*

memory, they can quickly and accurately identify people they know from a distance by their walk, posture, voice, and body outline.

Associative memory is a powerful device that allows us to make connections between fragmented data. It permits us to take advantage of analogies and to apply knowledge learned in one situation to a new set of circumstances. Unfortunately, associative memory runs into problems in areas like the multiplication tables, where various pieces of information must be kept from interfering with each other.

Devlin (2000) points out that when it comes to the multiplication tables, associative memory can cause problems. That's because we remember the tables through language, causing different entries to interfere with each other. A computer has no problem detecting that $6 \times 9 = 54$, $7 \times 8 = 56$, and $8 \times 8 = 64$ are separate and distinct entities. On the other hand, the brain's strong pattern-seeking ability detects the rhythmic similarities of these entities when said aloud, thus making it difficult to keep these three expressions separate. As a result, the pattern 6×9 may activate a series of other patterns, including 45, 54, 56, and 58 and load them all into working memory, making it difficult to select the correct answer.

Likewise, Dehaene (1997) stresses the problems that come with memorizing addition and multiplication tables. He notes that arithmetic facts are not arbitrary and independent of each other. Rather, they are closely intertwined linguistically, resulting in misleading rhymes and confusing puns. The following example is similar to one Dehaene uses to illustrate how language can confuse rather than clarify.

Suppose you had to remember the following three names and addresses:

- Carl Dennis lives on Allen Brian Avenue
- Carl Gary lives on Brian Allen Avenue
- Gary Edward lives on Carl Edward Avenue

Learning these twisted combinations would certainly be a challenge. But these expressions are just the multiplication tables in disguise. Let the names Allen, Brian, Carl, Dennis, Edward, Frank, and Gary represent the digits 1, 2, 3, 4, 5, 6, and 7, respectively, and replace the phrase "lives on" with the equal sign. That yields three multiplications:

- $3 \times 4 = 12$
- $3 \times 7 = 21$
- $7 \times 5 = 35$

From this perspective, we can now understand why the multiplication tables present such difficulty when children first encounter them. Patterns interfere with each other and cause problems.

Pattern interference also makes it difficult for our memory to keep addition and multiplication facts separate. For example, it takes us longer to realize that $2 \times 3 = 5$ is wrong than to realize that $2 \times 3 = 7$ is false because the first result would be correct under addition. Back in 1990, studies by Miller (1990) were already revealing that learning multiplication facts interfered with addition. He discovered that students in third grade took more time to perform addition when they started learning the multiplication tables, and errors like $2 + 3 = 6$ began to appear. Subsequent studies confirm that the consolidation of addition and multiplication facts correctly into long-term memory continues to be a major challenge for most children.

Over millions of years, our brain has evolved to equip us with necessary survival skills. These include recognizing patterns, creating meaningful connections, and making rapid judgments and inferences, even with only a smattering of information. Rudimentary counting is easy because of our abilities to use language and to denote a one-to-one correspondence with finger manipulation. But our brains are not equipped to manipulate the arithmetic facts needed to do precise calculations, such as multiplication, because these operations were not essential to our species' survival. Studies of the brain using electroencephalographs (EEGs) show that simple numerical operations, such as number comparison, are localized in various regions of the brain. But multiplication tasks require the coordination of several widespread neural areas, indicating a greater number of cognitive operations are in play (Micheloyannis, Sakkalis, Vourkas, Stam, & Simos, 2005). Consequently, to do multiplication and precise calculations, we have to recruit mental circuits that developed for quite different reasons.

> *Our brains are not equipped to manipulate the arithmetic facts required for precise calculations. To do arithmetic, we need to recruit mental circuits that developed for different reasons.*

The Impact of Language on Learning Multiplication

If memorizing arithmetic tables is so difficult, how does our brain eventually manage to do it? One of our strongest innate talents is the ability to acquire spoken language. We have specific brain regions in the frontal and temporal lobes that specialize in handling language. Faced with the challenge of memorizing arithmetic facts, our brain responds by recording them in verbal memory, a sizable and durable part of our language processing system. Most of us can still recall items in our verbal memory, such as poems and songs, that we learned many years ago.

Teachers have long recognized the power of language and verbal memory. They encourage students to memorize items such as rhymes and the multiplication tables by reciting them aloud. As a result, calculation becomes linked to the language in which it is learned. This is such a powerful connection that people who learn a second language generally continue to do arithmetic in their first language. No matter how fluent they are in the second language, switching back to their first language is much easier than relearning arithmetic from scratch in their second language.

Brain imaging studies carried out by Dehaene and his colleagues provided further proof that we use our language capabilities to do arithmetic. Their hypothesis was that exact arithmetic calculations involved the language regions of the brain because it required the verbal representations of number. Estimations requiring approximate answers, however, would not make use of the language facility (Dehaene et al., 1999).

The subjects of the experiments were adult English-Russian bilinguals who were taught two-digit addition facts in one of the two languages and were then tested. When both the teaching and the test question were in the same language, the subjects provided an exact answer in 2.5 to 4.5 seconds. If the languages were different, however, the subjects took a full second longer to provide the exact answer. Apparently, the subjects used that extra second to translate the question into the language in which the facts had been learned. When the question asked for an approximate answer, the language of the question did not affect the response time.

During the experiment, the researchers monitored the subjects' brain activity (Figure 5.6). Questions requiring exact answers primarily activated the same part of the left frontal lobe where language processing occurs. When the subjects responded to questions requiring approximate answers, the greatest activity was in the two parietal lobes, the regions that contain number sense and support spatial reasoning. Amazingly, these findings reveal that we humans are able to extend our intuitive number sense to a capacity to perform exact arithmetic by recruiting the language areas of our brain.

If you need more personal evidence of this connection between language and exact arithmetic, try multiplying a pair of two-digit numbers while reciting the alphabet aloud. You will find that this is quite difficult to do because speaking demands attention from the same language areas required for mental computation and reasoning.

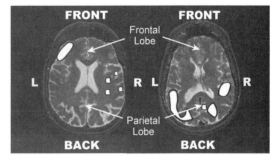

Figure 5.6 These composite fMRI scans show that exact calculations (left image) primarily activate language areas in the left frontal lobe, where verbal representations of numbers are processed. During approximate calculations (right image), the greatest activation was in the two parietal lobes that house number sense and support spatial reasoning (Dehaene et al., 1999).

> Because the language and number processing areas of the brain are separate, teachers should not assume that students with language problems will necessarily encounter difficulties with computation, and vice versa.

Yet despite this seeming cooperation between the language and mathematical reasoning areas of the brain, it is still important to remember that these two cerebral areas are anatomically separate and distinct. Further proof of this separation comes from case studies showing that one area can function normally even when the other is damaged (Brannon, 2005). Teachers, then, should not assume that students who have difficulty with language processing will necessarily encounter difficulties in arithmetic computation, and vice versa.

Do the Multiplication Tables Help or Hinder?

They can do both. Remember that children come to primary school with a fairly developed, if somewhat limited, sense of number. Thanks to their brain's capacity to seek out patterns, they can already subitize, and they also have learned a pocketful of simple counting strategies through trial and error. Too often, as noted above, arithmetic instruction in the primary grades purposefully avoids recognizing these intuitive abilities and resorts immediately to practicing arithmetic facts.

If the children's introduction to arithmetic rests primarily on the rote memorization of the addition and multiplication tables and other arithmetic facts (e.g., step-by-step procedures for subtraction), then their intuitive understandings of number relationships are undermined and overwhelmed. In effect, they learn to shift from intuitive processing to performing automatic numerical operations without caring much about their meaning.

On the other hand, if instruction in beginning arithmetic takes advantage of the children's number sense, subitizing, and counting strategies by making connections to new mathematical operations, then the tables become tools leading to a deeper understanding of mathematics, rather than an end unto themselves.

Some students may have already practiced the multiplication tables at home. My suggestion would be to assess how well each student can already multiply single-digit numbers. Then introduce activities using dots or pictures on cards that help students practice successive addition (the underlying concept of multiplication). The idea here is to use the students' innate sense of patterning to build a multiplication network without memorizing the tables themselves. Of course, this may not work for every student, and for some, memorizing the tables may be the only successful option.

WHAT'S COMING?

People are born with a number sense that helps them to determine the numerosity of small collections of objects and to do rudimentary counting, addition, and subtraction. How can we take advantage of these intuitive skills to help them learn more complex mathematical operations? What is current research in cognitive neuroscience telling us about how the brain learns, and how should we use this information when considering effective instruction in mathematics? These are some of the questions that get answered in the next chapter.

Chapter 5 — Learning to Calculate

Reflections

Jot down on this page key points, ideas, strategies, and resources you want to consider later. This sheet is your personal journal summary and will help to jog your memory.

6

The Male and the Female Brain

Abigail Norfleet James

SOURCE: Photographer: Duane Berger. Used with permission.

One side of a discussion about cognitive gender differences assumes that those differences will have an effect on how the individual processes information. If people have strong verbal skills, they are likely to read and listen well. People who have good spatial skills may find it easier to learn if the information is presented in a chart or graph. Most individuals can learn in a variety of ways, but a good number of us have preferred methods. The way the individual prefers to process information will determine what avenue will result in the most efficient learning.

Are there gender-specific approaches to learning? See how well you do in answering the following questions about how males and females learn differently.

QUIZ

Respond to the following statements by indicating whether the statement best describes (a) girls, (b) boys, or (c) both girls and boys.

1. Are more likely to be identified as generally learning disabled

2. Are more likely to be identified with a math disability

3. Are effectively able to define a problem and select the appropriate strategy

4. Spend more time after school on homework or studying

5. Learn best with peers because of their orientation to others

6. Have peer groups that are less likely to be study oriented

7. Have better proofreading skills

8. Are more willing to check for errors and correct mistakes

9. Are less likely to use a variety of strategies to solve problems

10. Have a more realistic view of academic success and failure

Answers are on pages 125–126.

Some teachers may not be completely persuaded that variations in the ways that girls and boys learn are based on cognitive gender differences. Their doubts may be based on the belief that girls and boys learn the way that they do because they were taught to study in a certain way. Certainly, that is part of the picture, but having taught in both girls' and boys' schools, I am convinced that many of the ways that children choose to learn are the result of their individual experiences in the classroom molded by their underlying cognitive gender differences. That means teachers need to be responsive to gender differences when planning academic activities, keeping in mind that what works for the teacher may not work for the student.

As a female with a brain that functions in many respects more like a male brain, I have learned not to assume that the sex of the child is necessarily indicative of how the child approaches learning. My learning disabilities are more similar to the boys I have taught than to the girls; I am terrible at spelling and auditory processing, which means that can I relate to many of the problems that my male students have in school. However, I am female, and my verbal abilities are more similar to those of my female students, so I understand some about how they approach academic work. Few of us are entirely one way or the other, and you will find some students whose way of working resembles the descriptions that follow and others who don't fit at all. Overall, you will find that more of your female students will match than not.

LEARNING MODALITIES

In this context, modality is a term that indicates the sensory sources of information, so learning modalities refer to learning when the source is ears (auditory), eyes (visual-verbal and visual-iconic), and hands (kinesthetic).

- Auditory learning occurs when the information is *heard.* Sources of auditory information are lectures, movies, seminars, small-group work, debates, or anytime that the individual is listening to information—actually, this involves much of what goes on in a classroom.
- Visual-verbal learning occurs when the information is *read.* Sources of visual-verbal information are books; handouts; information written on a blackboard, whiteboard, or SMART Board; PowerPoint presentations; or anytime that the individual is reading words.
- Kinesthetic learning occurs when the information is *manipulated.* Sources of kinesthetic information are lab exercises, taking notes, acting, singing, working problems, building models, conducting research, or anytime the individual is doing something with the material.
- Visual-iconic learning occurs when the information is *seen* but words are not central to the presentation of the information. Sources of visual-iconic information are charts, tables, graphs, pictures, demonstrations, movies, or anytime that the individual sees information presented in a pictorial or graphic fashion.

Auditory Learning

There is not a lot of research in this area, but it would seem that if a student easily accesses information through one of the sensory systems, that will be a good learning approach for that student. We know that girls' hearing is more acute than boys, so auditory information should be easier for girls to remember, and we have already seen that girls have better auditory memory than boys (Geffen, Moar, Hanlon, Clark, & Geffen, 1990; Vuontela et al., 2003).

There is a confounding factor in the statement, "Girls have better auditory memory," because what may actually be assessed is verbal memory. If the material to be remembered is presented in words, there is always the possibility that it is not the auditory but the verbal nature of the information that is the source of the female advantage in remembering what is heard. Because most information heard in a classroom involves words, teachers may believe that most female students will have better auditory memory than male students. However, as a female with lousy auditory memory, please know that if a student can't tell you what you just said, it may not be because the student wasn't paying attention but because the student doesn't remember auditory information, even though the information involves words. Believe me, there is a difference, and if I'm going to remember what I hear, I have to write it down. What this means for teachers is that verbal presentation of information is a good method to teach girls, but not all girls.

SUGGESTIONS FOR APPLYING THE THEORY TO YOUR CLASSROOM

✓ Make sure that you provide written directions or explanations no matter how clear you think you are in describing what the students are expected to do. Students who have poor auditory-processing skills will need to have another source to make sure that they get the information.

  o For young students, you will need to post directions or write them on the board.
  o For older students, you may use a website as a source of information. You can post homework assignments, extra material, links to other websites, and a lot of other information that can be read.

✓ Teach all students to take competent notes. Even if a female student is a good auditory learner, she will need to know how to convert information from an auditory source to a written record.

  o For young students, start by giving directions and asking the students to write down a summary of the directions. This will help you discover if any children have subtle hearing problems or auditory processing issues, but also, it gives children practice in getting the gist of what the teacher says, not necessarily the exact words.
  o Older girls will typically prefer to take notes in a linear fashion; however, some may be more visual and will relate better to webbing or charting. If you are not familiar with these techniques, ask the learning specialist in your school for assistance.
  o Although reading to students may not seem to be part of a math and science curriculum, giving students practice in listening will help develop auditory skills. In science, you might read about an animal and then have students draw a picture of it. By asking students to use nonverbal skills, you help students develop all of the means of acquiring information.

Verbal Learning

We discussed previously that the source of the female verbal advantage may be the result of their earlier left-sided brain development. Girls read earlier than boys and with greater confidence, although, certainly, you are going to find girls who have trouble reading in middle school and boys who are facile readers before they get to kindergarten. Frequently, what you will find is that girls will want to read about any topic you introduce in class in preference to any other method of acquiring information (Buck & Ehlers, 2002), so make sure that students have access to the material in written form.

SUGGESTIONS FOR APPLYING THE THEORY TO YOUR CLASSROOM

✓ Introduce material through verbal means: provide written information, tell a story, describe the material, and so forth.

✓ Act as a scribe for very young students to enable them to put into words an event or experience in class. Part of that exercise is developing their vocabulary, which helps them describe visual events.

✓ If the information is graphically presented or demonstrated to the class, make sure that you give a running commentary so that the girls have words to associate with the picture or visually presented material.

✓ If you teach young children, do not assume that all girls are facile readers. The girl who is a poor reader will be uncomfortable if she is identified by the class as having problems with reading. Make sure that she gets help in an unobtrusive way. If you have students read out loud in class, let this student prepare a passage in advance. No one has to know that the student was already familiar with the material.

Kinesthetic Learning

Kinesthetic learning tends to be more difficult for girls, as many are not inclined to manipulate materials. I found it difficult to get my female students to examine the parts of plants and reluctant to dissect specimens in a biology lab exercise. They would rather look at pictures in a book or look at someone else manipulating the material. Research supports that, in a science laboratory, girls were less likely to use tools in a novel way and more likely to follow carefully the directions of the teacher (Jones et al., 2000). However, once my students got used to laboratory exercises, they enjoyed them and learned a great deal through that method. I did not push them, but I did not do the dissections for them.

One reason girls may be less inclined to manipulate materials in class may be because of their lower level of impulsivity when compared to boys of the same age. There is lots of evidence that boys are more impulsive and are more likely to get physically involved in a class activity (Baron-Cohen, 2003; Honigsfeld & Dunn, 2003). It may be that in a coed classroom, girls are less inclined to become actively involved because the boys are so involved. In single-sex math classes, girls reported that they were better able to learn math because their greater involvement helped them become more comfortable with the material. The boys in the same study did not find that the single-sex format made a difference in their math performance (Seitsinger, Barboza, & Hird, 1998).

This is somewhat surprising given the fact that girls have better fine-motor skills earlier than boys (Kimura, 2000), so it might seem that girls would be more willing to touch and handle materials in the classroom. One reason for girls' preference for not interacting physically with class materials comes from the belief that girls are more willing to please the teacher (Maccoby, 1998; Pomerantz, Altermatt, & Saxon, 2002), and if the teacher says, "Don't touch," girls are more likely to obey. Another reason is that boys are more impulsive (James, 2007) and may simply take over the lab exercise.

SUGGESTIONS FOR APPLYING THE THEORY TO YOUR CLASSROOM

✓ Encourage girls to become physically involved with the manipulatives of a class exercise. In a coed class, you can divide students into groups by gender, but if you would prefer not to, provide some guidelines for a minimum amount of interaction with the material.

  ○ Younger students may be more willing to become physically involved in a class exercise. Keep watch to make sure that the girls are an active part of the assignment. If girls consistently let boys take over, assign specific tasks for each child in the group.

  ○ For older students, be careful that a girl does not always volunteer to be the scribe as her major contribution to the group effort. The rest of the students may be perfectly happy to let her do so. All students, even those with bad handwriting, need to learn to write down results or information from research.

✓ Make sure that if you use manipulatives in a math class that all students are taking part, as some girls may be tempted simply to observe others. Keep a chart of student interactions, and make sure that at least once each week each female student demonstrates to you that she is able to use the manipulative being studied.

✓ For upper-level science courses, have a lab-practical exam as part of the grade for the course. This will show students that it is important for them to get involved in the lab exercises and will allow students who are good at these skills a place to shine.

Visual Learning

Although most girls will remember well what they read, their memory for what they see is not as clear-cut. There is information that indicates that males are better at visual memory and visual learning in general (Martins et al., 2005), although other information implies that visual memory in girls matures before that of boys (Vuontela et al., 2003). The latter study may provide an explanation for the observation that women are clearly faster than men at perceptual speed, which is the ability to compare shapes and patterns such as letters, numbers, or pictures (Kimura, 2000). Here, visual memory is used as the individual scans the designs to remember what the target looks like to find the similar one. This skill is used to find differences between two similar pictures or to proofread. One theory is that women assign names to each of the symbols or designs and, therefore, turn a visual-memory task into a verbal one.

Some tests of visual memory, such as memory for object locations, have shown an advantage for women (Halpern, 2000). However, these results are not clear and other research shows that men may be better in object location than women (Cattaneo, Postma, & Vecchi, 2006; de Goede, Kessels, & Postma, 2006). If the information is presented graphically, it is likely that men will remember more material (Geiger & Litwiller, 2005). Men seem to have better visuospatial memory, a skill useful in computer games, as it involves movement in space and time; in one study, men were better able to determine what shape will result when two separate shapes are combined (Lawton & Hatcher, 2005).

Figure 6.1   Test of Visuospatial Memory

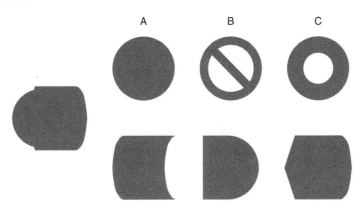

When combined, which set of shapes (A, B, or C) will result in the shape at the left?

Why am I interested in how well girls remember things other than words? In working with my students, I have found that remembering graphic and iconic data can be difficult for some girls—or at least they believe that it is difficult for them to remember such information. Part of the problem that some girls have with beginning algebra in particular is that they find the notation bewildering. First, the mix of numbers and letters to stand for variables is confusing—what does $4x$ stand for? To a verbally oriented student, the most important part of that term may be the letter, which should have some connection to a word, but here it plainly doesn't. Some girls find the repetitive use of x and y for variables confusing, especially if two successive problems use the same notation for unknowns.

SUGGESTIONS FOR APPLYING THE THEORY TO YOUR CLASSROOM

✓ If a girl is having trouble recognizing that the letters stand for variables, use your pencil to make a mark across each similar variable. Marking the variables is something I only do with students who are having trouble, and then only long enough for them to understand that the letters are standing for variables.

✓ Another strategy is to use a highlighter to make a dot over similar variables. Using different colors can be very useful when the problems involve more than one variable. For example,

○ $22 - 3x = 8x$ for one-variable equations, or
○ $3x + 4y = 12 - 2y + 2x$ for two-variable equations.

✓ Approach mathematical and scientific symbols as pictures that can show what it is they represent rather than mixed up letters. For example, the formula for sugar is $C_6H_{12}O_6$. Draw the hexagonal shape of the molecule so that the students can see how the letters and numbers fit together.

✓ In math, bring in real apples and oranges (or anything to stand in for different objects) and arrange them as in the equation. In the example earlier, use small blocks to stand in for the numbers. Use a big block for the variable and little blocks for the numbers. Put out the blocks as indicated in the problem—22 little blocks, 3 big blocks, and 8 big blocks. Let the students move the blocks around until they can see what value each big block has to have to make the equation work.

I have also found that some of my female students, particularly those in pre-algebra, find the symbols for operations baffling especially when the material gets beyond basic arithmetic terms. For example, what does -4 mean? Does that mean that you are to subtract four from something else, or does it mean that the value of the term is less than zero? How do you read -4? Is it minus four or negative four? The verbal descriptions are not the same as one indicates an operation and the other indicates a value. To an individual who focuses on words, that creates a problem. To someone who focuses on the numbers, it doesn't matter whether you are subtracting a quantity or whether that quantity has a negative value, as the effect is pretty much the same in a simple add/subtract equation. If a quantity is being multiplied by or divided by -4, then some students may have trouble understanding that the sign of the number indicates a value and not an operation.

One day, a student interrupted the lesson in class when she asked what the difference was between minus and negative. I pointed out that subtracting a positive four or adding a negative four gave the same result. She was still confused, and when I realized that the whole class was having problems with this at some level, I put a number line at the top of the board. I used it to help clarify each instance of this situation as it came up in the material until they all got comfortable with the ambiguous terminology. As you clarify this ambiguity, make sure that your students are comfortable with both meanings of the term as there are places when either one or the other is needed. For one pre-algebra class that was having particular trouble, I required them all to put a number line at the top of every test and use it to determine how to combine numbers until they were all able to do so easily.

Here is the crux of the matter, some terms in math and science are indeed ambiguous, and that creates difficulties for a student who is word oriented. Minus and negative are simply the tip of the iceberg. How about multiply and times? Is there a difference between twice and multiply by two or divide by and divide into? Does the delta symbol indicate change or heat? If a student remembers words best, the student needs to be clear on what the words mean. If girls have trouble with the symbols in math, they will ask questions such as, "What does that letter stand for?" or "Why does this problem use the same letters as an earlier problem? Do they have the same meaning or value?"

The research on memory and object location also gives a clue as to why some girls have trouble with the more graphic nature of math and science. If the reason women remember the location of objects is that they give names to the objects, then remembering the formula for glucose, which is $C_6H_{12}O_6$, may be difficult unless the formula is introduced as "Carbon six, hydrogen twelve, oxygen six." When I taught science in a girls' school, I always said the full name of each element as I wrote the formula on the board. I found it helped some of my students to be reminded of the names of the elements, even though we wrote $C_6H_{12}O_6$. As they became more familiar with the formulas, I just read what I wrote and did not give the full name of each element.

SUGGESTIONS FOR APPLYING THE THEORY TO YOUR CLASSROOM

✓ Do not be tempted to shortcut the names of terms when you write them until you are sure that every student in the class understands what you mean. While helping a girl learn to balance chemical equations, I discovered that she had no idea what the arrow meant (you will remember that it indicates a chemical reaction occurs).

✓ For students who are having trouble remembering the meaning of symbols, have them develop a chart or list of the symbols with their meaning. Do not be tempted to do this for them; it is making the list that helps them remember what the symbols stand for.

✓ Use physical objects, such as blocks, to stand in for variables in equations to help students understand what x stands for in an equation.

GROUP SIZE

When I talk to teachers about girls' group size, I usually get grins and lots of examples of what happens when you put an odd number of girls together to work on a project. Teachers are amazed when I tell them that there is research to back up their observations, and the research is very clear that girls work better in groups composed of even numbers. The reason given is that females focus on individuals in a group, so if they are in a group larger than two, the other people in the group may feel left out, as they are not receiving attention (Benenson & Heath, 2006). This is probably because of the focus on faces shown by infant girls, which was mentioned earlier.

If you have three girls working in a group, the likelihood is that two will focus on each other and the third student will not be included. Groups of four allow for pairs of girls to work together. I have seen three girls working together quite effectively, but it is the exception rather than the rule. If three girls ask to work together, give them the benefit of the doubt until you can observe whether all three are equal partners in the enterprise. I've also seen two girls who weren't very motivated or capable pick a lonely third girl who can do the work. The attention of the two is flattering to the one until she realizes that she is carrying the entire load.

SUGGESTIONS FOR APPLYING THE THEORY TO YOUR CLASSROOM

✓ If you need to have three girls work together, make sure that the tasks are well defined. That way, each student knows what she is to do and it will be obvious to all if one girl is trying to get someone else to do her work.

✓ If your class size requires that you use groups larger than two, make sure that the girls change groups on a regular basis. As new groups are started, girls will learn how to do different jobs. Also, if one group of girls is particularly toxic, moving students regularly will provide relief for the group that does not get along.

✓ It also helps to give two grades for group work, one grade for the project and another grade for individual effort. That will encourage all students to put forth a more equal amount of effort.

FAIRNESS

"It's not fair!" Every teacher has heard this complaint from students. Girls believe that effort is the measure of success, so a problem may occur if a child who spent three hours on an assignment gets a lower grade than a classmate who spent 20 minutes on the same assignment. The earlier all students learn that work is judged not on the amount of time spent preparing it but on the end result, the easier your task will be. This is another reason to grade with rubrics or other methods that clarify the standards for success.

In an attempt to help girls who focus on effort, teachers may give some credit or modify a grade when a student indicates that she spent a good deal of time preparing the assignment. Only do that if the rubric allows effort to improve a grade. Unless students learn this early, they may be surprised, particularly in college, when the teacher is only interested in the final product. I am convinced this is part of the issue that some girls have with math and science—the answer is the answer. The amount of time you spend getting it is not important. I have had girls tell me that they like courses where essay questions are given, as they believe that the teacher will give more points for longer answers—effort pays off.

Another issue with fairness is how rules are used to apply discipline. Girls believe that induction works best in dealing with misbehavior (Barnett, Quackenbush, & Sinisi, 1996). Induction is the method by which the adult or person in authority points out that another person has been hurt by the young offender and asks how the offender would feel if someone did the same thing to him or her. The focus of induction may center on how the misbehavior affects an adult, either parent or teacher—"I'm disappointed in your behavior"—or on how the misbehavior affects the victim—"How do you think that makes Suzie feel?" Girls feel that parent-oriented induction is more fair than victim-oriented induction (Horton, Ray, & Cohen, 2001). So not only do girls find induction a more fair way to discipline, but also they find that it is more fair to point out how the misbehavior affects the parent or other adult rather than the victim. The rules apply, but circumstances may mean that the application of the rules changes depending on the effect of the misbehavior. This is another instance of effort making a difference for girls.

For girls, fairness is a matter of listening to all sides and making the most equitable decision for all.

SUGGESTIONS FOR APPLYING THE THEORY TO YOUR CLASSROOM

✓ Rubrics for grading are essential in math and science, and they will make it much easier to help students see what they need to do and how their efforts are going to be graded. Give older students the rubrics for long-term assignments at the beginning so that they can see where to focus their efforts.

✓ Do not let students present work, especially lab reports, in elaborate report covers or in binders that are there for more than just keeping the work together. I have had subpar work presented with a very decorative cover in an attempt to suggest that the student spent a lot of time on the work. Most colleges do not allow work to be presented with more than a title page, and students need to get used to being graded on the content of the work and not on how it is displayed.

(Continued)

(Continued)

✓ Make sure that the rules in your class are very clear—posting them can help. At the beginning of the year, go over each rule and the reason for it. This will help later if a student claims not to understand a rule or that it is not "fair."

o For classes with younger students, the rules can be decided by having a guided discussion about what behavior helps the class to run well and respect all the members of the class.

o For classes with older students, rules can be determined by all the students in the class. In that case, post the rules and have each student sign the rules as an indication that she or he agrees to follow the rules. You can have a signed set of rules for each of your classes.

LEARNING DISABILITIES

There is no question that fewer girls are identified with learning disabilities than boys. Most learning disabilities involve language deficits, so it makes sense that the group whose language skills develop sooner are likely to have fewer problems. However, that does not mean that girls do not have learning disabilities, so if a student is not doing well in your class, the reason may be because of learning disabilities.

Children develop different skills at different rates, and schools should be sensitive to those differences. Do remember that what looks like a learning disability may actually be a difference in learning modality or difference in development. Those differences will still need to be addressed, but can be ameliorated by time or differences in teaching and approach.

Dyslexia

Dyslexia is any one of several different difficulties with language, and generally girls are diagnosed with such problems less often than boys. This group of disorders may involve problems with oral language, reading, or written language, and most individuals can learn, but usually in a way that is not typical in classroom instruction (Carreker, 2004). In light of the female verbal advantage, girls with dyslexia may be particularly sensitive to their learning problems because of the assumption that girls are not supposed to have trouble in this area.

The important factor here is to make sure the student is properly identified and receives the correct accommodations for her individual learning issues. Working with the special education teacher assigned to the child will help provide a learning environment where the student can thrive. You might help the child discover what she does know and figure out what means she used to acquire that information. Then assist the student to frame her schoolwork using similar methods. It is crucial to get the student to understand that she does learn, but perhaps the best way for her to learn is not the same way as most of the class. There are many ways to provide accommodations for the child with verbal learning issues, and the special education department at your school is the best source for help with specific strategies for each child.

SUGGESTIONS FOR APPLYING THE THEORY TO YOUR CLASSROOM

✓ For a girl in middle school for whom peer approval is important, being different may mean that that she is reluctant to be identified or singled out as having learning differences. Some girls may be embarrassed if others find out about their learning issues, and some students simply don't care. The problem is that accommodations may unmask her as learning disabled and that may be the reason she will not use the accommodations or allow you to do so.

✓ Very young girls may not be identified yet, so just because a student is not categorized as having dyslexia does not mean that she doesn't have it. One of my students with severe dyslexia was not identified until fourth grade because her spoken verbal skills were so good that it was hard to determine that her academic problems stemmed from her inability to read.

✓ Older students may find some support in talking to a senior female student or adult who has similar problems. Knowing that others have similar problems and have dealt successfully with them can be a great comfort.

✓ Many very prominent individuals are dyslexic. Have a girl do a report on such an individual paying particular attention to how that individual has coped with his or her learning difficulty.

Dysgraphia/Dyspraxia

Although the child with dyslexia has trouble getting information in, the child with dysgraphia has trouble producing information, particularly in writing. Dyspraxia is a more general term indicating difficulties with motor skills and coordination, including handwriting. Either diagnosis will mean that the child has trouble producing written work. The primary identifying characteristic of dysgraphia is poor handwriting, but the problem is far more complicated than that. Again, this is a problem where boys have more trouble, probably because of the combination of slower language skills together with later acquisition of fine motor skills. The child with dysgraphia will have trouble organizing thoughts on paper, will have a large gap between ideas communicated orally and written, will have difficulties with spelling and grammar, and will tire swiftly when writing (Dysgraphia, 2007). People with this problem will have trouble coordinating their hands to do different things at the same time, so playing the piano or a similar two-handed instrument will be difficult.

As a person with severe dysgraphia, I can attest to how much help the computer can be for children with this disorder. Although I tire quickly when writing anything by hand, I can type easily and rapidly, even though I have to say out loud what I am typing as I do so, which is why what I write sounds like I am talking to you. I had serious problems completing English compositions in school, but my son, who has the same problem, was started on a computer in the fourth grade and has far fewer problems. The important thing is to start accommodations early. Girls with dysgraphia should know that there might be a limit to how neat their handwriting can be, and they should be encouraged to use the computer. On the other hand, all children should be required to produce work that is at their level of neatness.

The move to make sure that all children are proficient on the computer may create some problems in the future. Research indicates that recognition of letters and characters, a skill necessary for reading, is promoted if the individual writes the letters as they are being learned (Longcamp et al., 2008; Longcamp, Boucard, Gilhodes, & Velay, 2006). Further, as all teachers know, handwriting has been shown to be an excellent way to learn vocabulary or other material (Naka, 1998). So even if typing is easier for me, I learned long ago that the best way for me to learn anything is to write it over and over, even in my bad handwriting. On the other hand, for writing original work such as essays or books, the computer is my friend.

SUGGESTIONS FOR APPLYING THE THEORY TO YOUR CLASSROOM

✓ Handwriting is not a popular topic to teach, although most small children like the repetitive exercises. Encourage your school or school system to make sure that handwriting is taught to all students.

✓ Make sure that students who have been identified with dysgraphia have ample opportunities to become familiar with the computer as that will assist them in producing neater work. The earlier the student can be properly identified, the more she can use technology to compensate for her difficulties in producing written work.

✓ Even though the student may use the computer to complete long assignments, all students should develop sufficient handwriting skills to write short notes or take down assignments. The new tablet computers provide great assistance for most students in taking notes, and mine has learned to read most of my handwriting!

✓ Girls with dysgraphia need help learning to structure essays using outlines or some other framework that will help them keep on track. Lab reports that have set formats are usually easier for them to complete. What is important is that the student understands that she will write better when she has a concrete structure to focus her efforts.

Dyscalculia

Dyscalculia is the "dys" of math. Although dyslexia and dysgraphia are more common in boys, dyscalculia affects girls and boys equally. Fairly recent information points to memory, specifically working memory, as the source of the problem (Kaufmann, Lochy, Drexler, & Semenza, 2004). Other models suggest that neuropsychological factors other than memory are the cause (Shalev, 2004). The problem is that because no one cause has been identified, treatments deal with symptoms rather than the root of the disorder. One of the most frustrating scenarios of teaching a child with dyscalculia occurs when the teacher spends a lot of one-on-one time to teach the child a specific skill in math and the child seems to master it. The next day, however, the child comes back to class with little or no memory of how to solve similar problems. When the disorder is seen as a specific memory issue or a neurological processing problem and not one of comprehension, it is easier to understand that the difficulty that the dyscalculic has with math can be managed.

I am competent in fairly complicated mathematics and have taught classes from pre-algebra to trigonometry. Yet I cannot calculate the tip for a waitress in my head. Yes, I can move the decimal over to take ten percent of the total; the problem comes when I cannot add two ten percents and the original amount without writing down the numbers. The best feature of my cell phone is the tip calculator! Knowing that my problem in math is a matter of memory makes a huge difference in my confidence that I can manage numbers. After years of making subtraction mistakes, I now justify my checkbook with a calculator. Helping a girl realize that her problem in math may be based on a memory deficit or a processing problem rather than an inability to understand the process may help her be more willing to keep working in math.

SUGGESTIONS FOR APPLYING THE THEORY TO YOUR CLASSROOM

✓ Some help is available at www.ldonline.org. That website will assist you in providing methods for your student with dyscalculia to manage her problems in math.

✓ The sooner students' problems in math can be attributed to dyscalculia, the sooner they can begin to use methods to compensate. I've counted on my fingers all my life and I have a calculator with me all the time. All students need to learn the basic facts of math and good retrieval of information from the multiplication tables will help students move more quickly through solving a problem.

✓ A chronic problem for the dyscalculic is reversal of numbers as problems are transferred from a source to a page where the work is to be done. You will give

(Continued)

(Continued)

students hope that they can do math if you will give part credit for those problems if the work is correct although the problem was written down wrong.

✓ A common accommodation is to allow the older dyscalculic students to bring formulas and other similar information to a test for math and science. One way for older students to do this is to program a graphing calculator with that information. Knowing that they don't have to remember those formulas will help the dsycalculic focus on doing the math rather than trying to remember the formulas.

SYNTHESIZING VERSUS ANALYZING

The female brain has been described as the synthesizing brain and the male brain as the analyzing brain (Baron-Cohen, 2003). Simon Baron-Cohen has described the different approaches by pointing out that "the female brain is predominantly hardwired for empathy. The male brain is predominantly hardwired for understanding and building systems" (p. 1). In the classroom, this means that girls need to see the whole picture and boys may be inclined to see the parts. In presenting material to girls, the effective teacher may start by giving the students an overview such as, "Let's look at the table of contents and see where our book is going to take us this year."

Don't forget, some of the girls in your class will have an analyzing approach and some of the boys will have a synthesizing approach to learning. That means that you need to provide both approaches whether or not your class is coed.

SUGGESTIONS FOR APPLYING THE THEORY TO YOUR CLASSROOM

✓ Girls tend to take a very personal approach to learning, which can be very effective as we all find information easier to learn as it applies to us. However, anything you can do to help them objectify what they learn, even in a small way, will help girls understand how anything is put together.

  o Encourage young girls to work with building blocks. Generally the boys tend to monopolize those toys, so put some aside for girls to work with. Have them build a dollhouse or a scale model of the classroom.

  o Have students use tiles to follow pictures of patterns. Mosaics are an excellent way to build a whole picture by focusing on the details.

✓ If girls tend to look at the big picture, you may need to help them see the building blocks.

  o With young students, have them draw the steps in the water cycle. Then have them cut the steps apart. Have them draw a picture of the earth with clouds above and then put the pieces of the water cycle in the correct places.

  o In science, older students might understand the basic functions that are performed by a cell, but not be sure of exactly which organelles are responsible for those functions and exactly what is happening. Have the students draw a picture of each organelle down the side of a page and then write the specific function next to the picture. Organelles that work together to perform a function could be color-coded to make them stand together.

LEARNING DIFFERENCES AND THE CLASSROOM

When we learn material, each of us approaches that learning opportunity from the way that makes the most sense to us. That viewpoint is probably shared by many others, but not by all. In the teaching process, if the teacher and learner do not share similar approaches to the material, it may be difficult for the learner to understand what is being taught. It is important for teachers to present information using different learning approaches to maximize the impact that the material has on the students in the class.

In Chapter 8, you will find a brief assessment to determine the preferred learning modalities for your students. They may be interested in finding out this information and learning how best to frame their study approaches.

ANSWERS TO QUIZ

1. B—Boys are more likely to be identified as generally learning disabled, especially true for language-based disabilities. Recent information indicates that such identification may not reflect a teacher bias but indicates that boys have more learning disabilities than girls (Linderman, Kantrowitz, & Flannery, 2005).

2. C—There is no gender difference in dyscalculia, the learning disability in math. There is an equal chance for a girl or a boy to suffer from this disorder (Lachance & Mazzocco, 2006).

3. A—Girls, ages 5 to 17, are better at planning or defining a problem and selecting the appropriate strategy than their male peers (Naglieri & Rojahn, 2001).

(Continued)

(Continued)

4. A—Girls spend more time studying and doing homework after school. Boys are much more likely to be engaged in sports and play both indoors and outdoors (Du, Weymouth, & Dragseth, 2003; National Center for Educational Statistics [NCES], 2007).

5. B—Boys are very peer oriented and learn better in a collegial atmosphere with other boys than with their teacher (Honigsfeld & Dunn, 2003; Pyryt, Sandals, & Begoray, 1998).

6. B—Boys, even though they learn best in groups, their groups are frequently not academically oriented (Van Houtte, 2004).

7. A—Girls have better proofreading skills. This is related to the skill of perceptual speed and women are faster at comparing symbols and designs (Kimura, 2000; Naglieri & Rojahn, 2001).

8. A—Girls are more willing to check for errors and correct mistakes. Perceptual speed is involved here, but the willingness to do this may be a factor of girls being less impulsive or wanting to be successful (Stumpf, 1998).

9. B—Boys will continue to use familiar strategies even if the method is not successful (Stumpf, 1998).

10. A—Girls are convinced that academic success is tied to the effort expended, but they are better able to be realistic about their progress (Tibbetts, 1977).

7

The Special Needs Brain

Eric Jensen

T his book sets up what educators call "differences" in kids. There are primarily two different categories, or operating systems, explored in this book: social and academic. The framework for understanding each empowers you as the educator to think about what is different in the brain. This operating system model is less about figuring out what's wrong with a "broken" brain and more about simply understanding a differences model that needs to work well in the context of school. As we delve into these differences, you will see that there is little overlap in the specific subskills of each operating system. But the basic concept is the same—when this system is impaired, the student has problems.

THE BRAIN'S SOCIAL OPERATING SYSTEM

A child's social-emotional operating system is actually quite complex. In fact, you could dream up quite a long list of attitudes, skills, and so on that students need to have in order to socialize properly in school, some of which can be taught quickly or managed through socialization (e.g., waiting their turn in line, keeping their hands off others, responding to social cues with appropriate behavior). But only a few core skills are needed to succeed.

The Social Brain Can Be Rewired With Experience

While many areas of the brain are involved in social capacities, we'll focus on six primary systems: sensory awareness, social reasoning, theory of mind, affiliation and empathy, emotional states, and reward evaluation (see Figure 7.1). When you build the subskills of these systems, you strengthen the brain in ways that will provide lasting gifts. These subskills truly enable students to get a leg up in life because good social skills are high on the list of what matters most.

The relevance of understanding these subskills is simple: when students have social and behavioral issues, one or more of these six factors is not up to the level needed to succeed in school. That does not mean the student is "broken." It simply means that one of the contributing brain patterns of social success is not working well for success in a school environment. For example, many adults with high-functioning Asperger syndrome can do quite well finding a job and earning a living in society, but kids with this syndrome struggle in a school-based environment that is highly cooperative because their brains don't process social information well. This does not mean, however, that they can't succeed in school. They have a different brain, not a broken one. Most gaps can be filled, and new skills can be learned. It simply takes understanding and patience. All kids can learn; educators must have the will, time, and the resources to make that happen.

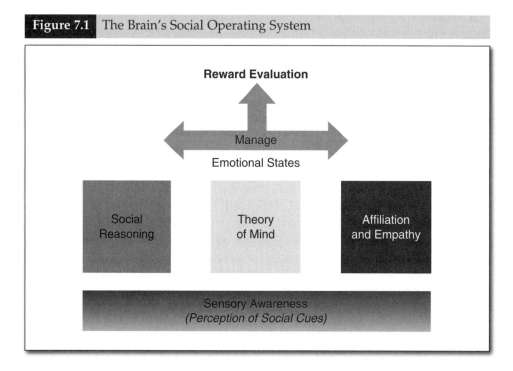

Figure 7.1   The Brain's Social Operating System

When any part of this operating system is not functioning well, there are various strategies you can use to strengthen it. (See Table 7.1 also, for resources to consult for additional ideas.)

Sensory Awareness. This area deals with perception and accurate processing of relevant social cues. Develop these skills through role-plays, direct instruction, and follow-up discussion.

STRATEGIES: In class, use case studies of common student scenarios and engage students in cooperative small-group work to teach them to think differently about how to behave. Watch a DVD as a class, and discuss what happened and what could be done different.

Social Reasoning. This involves the capacity to make decisions with others in mind, gain acceptance within a given group, and manage the effects of peer pressure.

STRATEGIES: Teach listening skills explicitly as part of a cooperative learning activity. Students need to be part of a well-defined and well-managed cooperative group to hear and see the effects of social behaviors and participate in developing social reasoning skills. Use case studies for older kids (Grades 5 and up). Use direct instruction coaching with all ages.

Theory of Mind. This is the capacity to put oneself in another's shoes in order to predict that person's likely actions and feel empathy for him or her.

STRATEGIES: This set of subskills can be enhanced by prediction activities in language arts and partner work that require students to make assumptions. Role-plays and case studies of highly typical student behaviors and scenarios are another great source for learning to predict another's mind set.

Affiliation and Empathy. These skills are defined by reliable, relational bonding with another person. Many students with disorders related to this area have had chaotic upbringings with insecure or hostile attachments.

STRATEGIES: This set of skills can be enhanced by experience and feedback with cooperative learning, teams, and other close-knit group time. It must be reinforced with team norms, feedback, and both teacher and peer assessments. Teach students how to form friendships and, more important, how to maintain them.

Emotional States. The capacity to manage one's own emotional states and purposefully influence those of others is very important. This can be developed best through long-term activities that have a chance to gain student interest and showcase varied responses.

STRATEGIES: Options for training the brain include drama, theater groups, role-plays, and writing fiction stories about people's lives. In addition, sports can help students learn to manage the feelings of winning and losing and recognize the value of good sportsmanship.

Reward Evaluation. This is the adaptive use of reciprocity—appropriate responsiveness to social signals with a healthy give and take. Positive social interactions can be very emotionally rewarding. But this is learned; it is not innate in the brain's wiring. The teacher needs to take a strong role here. Unless students have learned to get positive feelings from "please" and "thank you" as well as a host of other social cues such as smiles, handshakes, and hugs, it will be foreign to them.

STRATEGIES: Teach healthy give-and-take responses in class, and model them for all of your students. Don't tell students what to do; show them *how* to do it. This is typically modeled in the healthy family. Without that modeling at home, students can still learn it through classroom activities such as writing letters of gratitude to others.

As one might expect, many educators have difficulty teaching social skills to school-age children. Part of it is that the process is time intensive. It is also very different than teaching definitions, numbers, letters, or days of the week. There are multiple components, including syntax (the rules of language), semantics (the nonverbals and meaning behind actual words), and pragmatics (the situational use of social language). Without each part functioning, there will be difficulties. And it takes each of the six previously discussed parts of the model to ensure proper functioning. Otherwise, one cannot be a successful and complete communicator.

Table 7.1 Building Social Skills

Websites for Building Social Skills

Let's Face It! web.uvic.ca/~jtanaka/letsfaceit/activities.php

Posit Science, www.positscience.com

Social Skill Builder, www.socialskillbuilder.com/howtochoose.html

Second Life, secondlife.com

Longer-Term, In-Depth Programs to Build Social Skills

TeachTown.com

Natural Environment Teaching (NET)

Pivotal Response Training (PRT)

Prelinguistic Milieu Teaching (PMT)

Boardmaker

Laureate Learning Systems

SpeechTeach

Picture This

What you'll notice in the strategies offered in the next several chapters is that every one of them relates to these six core skills. These six skills are presented first because they provide the framework for understanding the rest of the strategies. For example, many students have a tough time being social or civil the moment stress levels go up, and students with oppositional disorder are among those most behaviorally challenged by increased stress. The emotional states factor discussed earlier speaks to this challenge. Only by learning stress-reducing strategies (e.g., reframing, taking deep breaths, seeing another's point of view, counting to 20) will students ever have a chance to get their lives back under control.

How to Maximize Results

Building the social operating system is a top priority. If a student is in an impoverished home environment for hours every day and then gets a few minutes of operating system enhancement at school, that time constitutes only a tiny fragment of the student's total week. That time is unlikely to produce substantial long-term benefits (though it's certainly better than nothing). The message here is clear: do not kid yourself about changing the brain—it takes time.

The human brain is highly susceptible to environmental input. In some cases, change—even permanent change—can happen within minutes. But that's likely to be a change induced by trauma (e.g., emotional, psychological, physical). To get lasting positive change, you'll want to go right up to the maximum time per day allowed by the brain, which on average is about 30 to 90 minutes of intensive skill building in any area. Beyond that, there's no evidence of gain. The brain just overloads, and the change is dismissed.

Let's translate this into your school time. To maximize change with skill building, students will have to be in a pullout situation. Why? Unless one follows the brain's rules for skill building, precious time is wasted, students learn less, and teachers get frustrated. The rules are simple (see Table 7.2).

However, as Chapter 1 revealed, there are other ways to get improvement without direct instruction in skill building. You can place a student in an enrichment (i.e., inclusion) classroom, but this is only valuable if two things take place: there is also pullout time for skill building each day, and the student is not highly disruptive to the class. In addition, you can facilitate growth indirectly through accommodations. This four-part system from Chapter 1 is repeated here because it is so powerful:

1. Always provide hope.

2. Organize as much skill building for the operating system as you can.

3. Create enrichment opportunities whenever possible.

4. Ensure that any needed accommodations are made.

Table 7.2	Skill-Building Rules

Learner must:

Buy into an activity

Perceive relevance

Get good sleep

Have focused attention

Activity must:

Be coherent to learners

Build in both positive and negative feedback

Last 30 to 90 minutes a day

Occur three to six times per week

Even if the conditions, resources, or policies are not ideal, take and use any of the suggested interventions that you can. The optimal ones, the ones that accelerate progress, use all four of these factors. The best interventions build an operating system because that's the most lasting change and it ripples across all areas of one's life.

THE BRAIN'S ACADEMIC OPERATING SYSTEM

Academic skills have a brain system that overlaps with social skills in the areas of awareness and attention. It's not a huge overlap, but there are some connections nonetheless. At school, the primary factors that interact, mitigate, or support the academic operating system are relationships, socialization, and social status. Each of these plays a part in the motivation, decision making, and cognition needed to succeed each day.

Students do not need to be superior in all of these areas to get good grades, but they do need enough of any compensatory strategies to succeed. The good news is that each of the critical processes in the brain's academic operating system is malleable, trainable, and can be improved.

The CHAMPS Mind Set

To make the brain system more memorable, I have labeled the academic operating system CHAMPS, an acronym that refers to a champion's mind set, hope, attention, memory, processing, and sequencing (see Figure 7.2).

Figure 7.2 The Brain's Academic Operating System

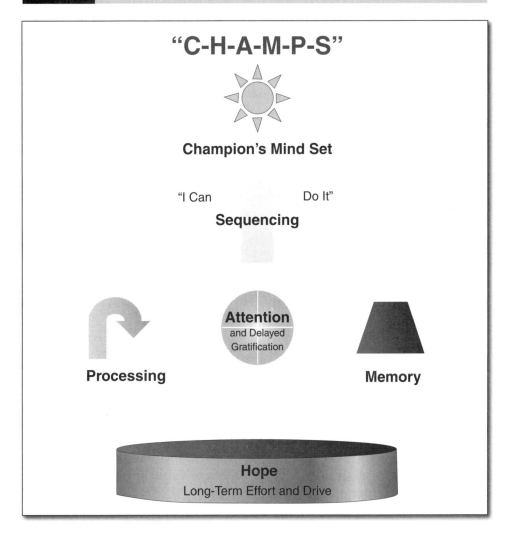

Let's consolidate what we know. Students are not stuck the way they are. Their success is dependent on their operating system, and it can be upgraded. For example, physical activity can increase a student's production of new brain cells (Pereira et al., 2007), and this is highly correlated with learning, mood, and memory. Playing chess can increase reading (Margulies, 1991) and math (Cage & Smith, 2000) capabilities by increasing attention, motivation, processing, and sequencing skills. Many arts can improve attentional and cognitive skills (Posner, Rothbart, Sheese, & Kieras, 2008). Using certain computer-aided instructional programs can, in just weeks, increase attention and improve working memory (Kerns, McInerney, & Wilde, 2001; Westerberg & Klingberg, 2007), both of which are significant upgrades to a student's operating system. Students are not stuck with poor attention span. Instead of demanding more attention in class, you can train students in how to build it with the following strategies.

Champion's Mind Set. This is the way of thinking that exudes confidence.

STRATEGIES: Give students genuine affirmations often, and support deserving student-to-student affirmations. Provide support for learning with tools, partners, and confidence. Create short assignments and opportunities for quick successes that tell the learners, "You can do it!" Help strengthen their social status by providing appropriate opportunities for privileges with their peers.

Hope. Hope is the voice that says, "There are better days ahead." It is fundamental for long-term effort. It requires deferred gratification and only works when there is something to be hopeful for. Students who have learned helplessness have a complete lack of hope, as do many with learning delays. But you can help change this.

STRATEGIES: Strengthen teacher-to-student relationships so that students know they have social support. Create situations in which students can experience success. Provide quality role models for success. Teach imagination, positive goal setting, and how to achieve those goals. Help students learn to manage their time and create checklists to manage their lives. Teach them how to make better choices, and give them practice at making choices. Ask them about their dreams, and let them draw, sing, talk, write, or rap about them.

Attentional Skills and Delayed Gratification. Paying attention is not an innate skill. What's innate is shifting attention from one novel attention grabber to another. It takes practice to learn to focus on the details over time. Students with attention deficit problems typically have focus and attention issues (among others).

STRATEGIES: Focus on high-interest arts content that allows students to immerse themselves in a situation requiring detailed focus. Build focus through high-interest reading. Build attention through focused practice in martial arts, dance, chess, model building, and sports. Helpful websites include fitbrains.com and playattention.com.

Memory. In school, a strong memory is not just expected, it is priceless. We are born with a good long-term memory for spatial learning, emotional events, procedural and skill learning, conditioned response learning, and highly behaviorally relevant data such as our phone number and the names of our siblings and parents. Outside of these, school learning requires both short-term memory and long-term faculties.

STRATEGIES: Practice with simple call-and-response in class. Build up to pair-share with partners. Strengthen memory with repetition, framing the importance of an idea. Teach students memory aids (e.g., mnemonics, loci method, peg systems, acronyms). Develop their skills in mind mapping.

Processing. This is the capacity to flesh something out. At the micro level, it means a student can process auditory input such as phonemes, which is quite important for reading. At the macro level, it means a student can process an event (e.g., being called a name, breaking up with a lover, forgetting to do homework). We all need to know how to deal with difficulties, particularly emotional ones. And we need to be able to ask appropriate questions and think critically about a problem. Kids with dyslexia or learning delays often have significant processing issues.

STRATEGIES: Provide verbal walk-throughs of class processes (e.g., "Now we are doing this . . . and next we'll need to. . . ."). Teach critical thinking and logic skills (specialized software can help with this). Offer challenging games with structured practice time. Encourage students to play a musical instrument or take drama classes; both will strengthen memory. Give students a partner so they can develop metaskills as they learn to talk through their thinking and acting process.

Sequencing. This is the set of skills that allow us to prioritize, identify, and put in order a set of actions. When you prepare a meal for guests, pack for a trip, or paint a bedroom, you need sequencing skills. At school, kids need these skills for starting homework, writing a paper, planning a project, resolving conflict, doing a math problem, and planning their day.

STRATEGIES: Experience and mentoring are the two best teachers for this skill set. Give students the opportunity to build things (e.g., models, paper projects, displays). Be the guide for each project to help set goals, organize materials, and use preteaching in organizing their work, writing a paper, or problem solving. Encourage them to get involved in the arts; most arts opportunities require attention, hope, processing, and sequencing.

Without an upgrade of these skills, your school will be doing more of the same and getting more of the same. When you upgrade students' systems for learning, you completely change the equation. In this book, you'll learn how to upgrade any student's impaired academic operating system, including those with problems in reading, math, and overall learning delays. When we address academic problems throughout the course of this book, it will always come back to strengthening students' academic operating systems. Stronger systems mean better performance.

Part III

Instructional Strategies for Every Brain

8

Calming the Brain

Michael A. Scaddan

Anything a learner perceives as stressful is!

The human brain's prime purpose is survival, the secondary purpose is meeting emotional needs, and the third is cognitive learning (Carter, 1998). Although some stress is necessary in the classroom as a motivator, only when high stress is minimized will the brain allow cognitive learning to take place (Dispenza, 2007; Howard, 2000).

High stress is a barrier to learning. It sends signals to the amygdala, the "flight and fight" response center in the brain, and reduces flow to the thalamus, which receives input from all senses except smell (Howard, 2000; Kutolak, 1997).

Stress reduces blood flow to the prefrontal cortex, the center for common sense and decision making (Jensen, 2006; Sapolsky, 1998). This is why the response to stress is not logical; it is emotionally based. It is also why asking a stressed person why she behaved in a certain way will often get an inadequate response. She probably doesn't know why. As far as she knows, the reaction just happened.

The negative impacts of high stress include these:

- impaired memory
- decreased ability to prioritize
- increased rote behavior
- damages to our immune system
- accelerated aging
- weakened ability to think creatively

In addition, high stress is more prevalent among minorities and low socioeconomic groups (Barr, 1997; Carter, 1998; Howard, 2000; Sapolsky, 1998).

Instead of regarding yourself as a teacher, look upon yourself as the person who sets the classroom "state." If the state is warm and secure, the possibility of positive learning occurring is heightened.

Teach anti-stress techniques such as these:

- Begin the day with warm-ups such as *talking circles* (circles where manipulatives are held while talking). This is an opportunity to shed emotional baggage.
- Introduce simple massage practices. This may begin with massaging your own shoulders or those of a friend. (This may not be appropriate in your school, but our teachers found it very effective.)
- Practice breathing techniques, tai chi, or yoga.
- Walk on the grass with bare feet to reduce static electricity.
- Drink filtered water, especially after exercise or computer work.
- Listen to peaceful music.
- Use affirmations that promote a state of calm.
- Allow reluctant readers to read through a finger puppet to lessen perceived stress.

Model behavior:

- Take the time to greet students upon arrival to class.
- Listen, really listen, to them by creating uninterrupted listening time (which may not be right now).
- Begin every day by reviewing the previous day's work through quizzes, mind maps, discussion, summaries, or active reviews. The brain works on patterns and connections rather than isolated incidents. This process provides the opportunity for connection to a theme through a daily or session overview. The ability to make strong, clear connections between learning situations aids understanding and thereby lowers stress.
- Eliminate sarcasm, ridicule, and name-calling. These are all power techniques that stress the brain. Embarrassment can result in the brain/body going through stress similar to a near death experience (Sapolsky, 1998).
- Allow sufficient time and provide resources for a given task.
- Provide overviews. This gives an opportunity for the "global" learners who need the big picture to see how the process works.
- Ensure that the students know what they are expected to learn, how they will be able to learn it, how they will know when they have learned it, and how the new knowledge or skill can be transferred into real life.
- Provide opportunities for movement and manipulative aids such as Koosh® balls[1].
- Allow students to learn through their preferred styles and demonstrate learning through varied intelligences.

One person's stress is another's celebration.

---

1. Koosh® is a registered trademark of ODDZON PRODUCTS, INC.

As a teacher entering a school that had already established effective brain-compatible teaching techniques, I began with something that I personally believed would make a difference with the eleven- to thirteen-year-old students in my class—daily morning shoulder massages. Although considered inappropriate in many schools, our school community was strongly in favor of adopting the practice after the parents and students consented. (The shoulder massages were only conducted in the presence of the teacher.) After some initial reluctance among students, the ritual grew to the point where it became a normal part of the day.

The real evidence that this was a great way to prepare for learning became apparent when outside activities interfered with the students' usual morning massage routine. They would request that the massage session be incorporated later in the day and often used it during DEAR (Drop Everything And Read) sessions that began after lunch.

As the ritual developed, reflection was added, with students telling their partners which massage technique was the best and why. Personal goal setting was also intro-duced as I, in my role as teacher, provided a quiet overview of the day's expectations.

Massage became a daily expectation for which the students took responsibility. This ensured that they received positive touch as well as reflection time and goal setting in a supportive environment.

An authorized massage can be a very important tool to use in the brain-compatible classroom. It encourages positive and caring touch, is a great state-change, incorporates relaxing or motivating music to assist in setting the tone, and can be used to break down social barriers that can be relevant to certain groups. Imagine how you would feel with a massage to begin each day.

SOURCE: Simon Drewery, former Te Puna teacher and now Principal of Waihi Central School, New Zealand

Brain-Based Review

You put the info in

to take the learning out.

You put reflection in,

and you shake it all about.

You do the "What, so now what?" and you use it soon.

That's what it's all about.

Review and reflection

gives the learning direction.

Review and reflection—

that's what it's all about.

This is the first verse of a review song that I wrote for the "Learn to Learn" program. As with all good learning, review and reflection are vital so let's review your progress.

1. Reminding students what your values are needs to be done regularly. How often do you plan to share "What you will do and what you will never do for them?" Discuss ideas with other adults, and you will gradually expand the number of values that you can share with students. We often don't realize that we have so many. I suggest that you write them down so you can use them again in the future. Maybe you could write them on a chart displayed in the classroom. These could be expanded to include your class's shared values.

2. At this stage of the year, the end of the fifth week and the fifth tool, there would be benefits in reviewing what you have covered so far and also any positive changes that you have noticed in your students' attitudes.

3. Once started, it is important that you continue to use the VIP every week so that it becomes part of the culture. Experiment with different presentation days and styles until you have a working model.

4. "You don't know this about me" could become a journal entry on a daily/weekly basis, growing instead to "I didn't know this about myself." In this way students can see specifically what they learned that day/week and how it changed them.

You keep it practical,

that cures many ills.

You put the music in

and include the movement, too.

You do the self assessment and the peer review.

That's what it's all about.

Review and reflection

gives the learning direction,

Review and reflection—

that's what it's all about.

9

Engaging the Brain

Marcia L. Tate

WHAT: CONNECTING TO REAL LIFE

How many times has a student asked you, "Why do we have to learn this?" That student was probably not being facetious and should not be penalized for sarcasm. If the purpose of the brain is to survive in the world, when students cannot see the connection between the lesson being taught and their world, the question will be asked. The answer is simple. Show the student the connection between what you are teaching and their world.

For example, if I were teaching elementary students the concept of main idea and details, I could use the simile of a table top and legs. I would open my lesson with the following *hook.*

> Class, look at the table in our classroom. The top of the table is supported by the four legs. A main idea in a story we will read must also be held up, or supported, by the details in the story. Let's draw a table with four legs. When we discover the main idea, we will write it on the top of our table. Then, we will find four supporting details to hold up that main idea and write one detail on each leg of our table.

A middle or high school lesson on main idea might open with the following *hook.*

> Class, how many of you have sent a text message to a friend on your cell phone? Well, today we are going to discuss why you need to recognize and form a main idea statement. You see, when you text message a friend, you are actually giving them the main idea, or gist, of your message. You cannot give them more of the details because that would be too expensive. Today, we are going to read several paragraphs and then stories where the main idea, or text message, is stated and we have to find it. Then, we will get so good at this concept that we will be able to formulate our own main ideas. We will then text message our original main ideas to one another.

With this opening to my lesson, I stand a better chance of attracting the attention of most, if not all, of my students and decreasing disruptions or classroom management concerns.

In the book *Worksheets Don't Grow Dendrites* (Tate, 2003), all 20 strategies work for the brain because they represent the ways in which human beings acquire and retain information. Several of the strategies, however, relate directly to relevant learning. They are as follows: field trips; manipulatives, experiments, labs, and models; project-based and problem-based instruction; technology; and work-study. Let's examine the relevance of each of these strategies.

When students take field trips they are able to travel to real places relevant to the content being studied. Even some of the greatest teachers in the world, such as Socrates and Aristotle, used the field trip as a major instructional tool (Krepel & Duvall, 1981). Take the field trip closer to the beginning of the unit of study so that the real-world connections can make the learning more comprehensible and memorable. In this day and age, teachers have an additional option: to take virtual field trips via modern technology.

When students use manipulatives, build models, perform experiments, or conduct labs, they are using their hands to connect with the world. This is why students often count on their fingers before they count in the abstract. A chemistry student who may have difficulty passing an objective paper-and-pencil test may well be capable of conducting the labs required for the course. These labs will help the student experience what real chemists actually do. Isn't it strange that in many classrooms throughout the country, lab work only counts for 20% or less of the overall grade, when real chemists spend more time performing labs than anything else?

Conducting real-world projects and solving real-life problems encourage active learning and discourage student passivity (Silver, Strong, & Perini, 2000). In fact, I bet you still remember a project in which you were engaged when you were in school. I still remember securing some water from the creek across the street from my house, bringing it to school in a baby food jar, and placing a drop of it under the microscope so that we could look for paramecia. When students solve problems, they also perceive the curriculum as more relevant.

The U.S. Secretary's Commission on the Acquisition of Necessary Skills (SCANS, 1991) report lists the ability to use technology as one competency that high school students must possess if they are to be prepared for the world of work. While the use of technology is a viable vehicle for effective instruction, using it as the sole means is problematic. The SCANS report also lists interpersonal skills as an essential competency. It is difficult for students to develop the essential social skills needed in the workplace if they are not provided with opportunities to do so in class. Another reason for the use of more active engagement strategies stems from the fact that as students sit in front of the computer, video games, and television, they develop a more sedentary lifestyle. As a result, the incidence of Type 2 diabetes is increasing at an alarming rate.

Work-study, apprenticeships, practica, and internships are viable tools for actively engaging students in meaningful and relevant curriculum, diminishing the number and frequency of behavior problems. Even in alternative schools throughout the nation, where student populations consists of those who have been suspended or expelled from traditional schools due to severe disciplinary infractions, work-study appears to be the order of the day. When I teach in these schools, I observe students involved in planting and tending gardens or preparing and serving meals. All students benefit when the academics are integrated into the relevant world of work.

WHY: THEORETICAL FRAMEWORK

For students to be motivated, they must perceive the subjects taught in school, such as reading, math, history, and science, as either necessary or desirable (Sprenger, 2005).

When students are actively engaged in art or science projects, problem-solving activities, and role-plays or simulations, they strengthen the thinking skills contained in the cerebellum (Feinstein, 2004).

The chances that new information will be remembered are increased when that information is connected to relevant issues (Sprenger, 2005).

Students disengage from learning when they do not perceive the relevance of it, are bored by it, or become stressed with it (Tileston, 2004).

Giving consideration to students' interests helps to guarantee that they can apply the standardized content they are learning to real life (Feinstein, 2004).

Students' self-systems (their attitudes, beliefs, and emotions) are directly influenced by their belief that the knowledge they are about to learn or the tasks they are about to complete are relevant to them and important to know and be able to do (Tileston, 2004).

When we impart information to students, their brains attempt to connect the new information to patterns previously stored. When there are no such connections, the new information can be lost (Sprenger, 2005).

Have students set personal goals for their learning and inquire often to make sure that they are meeting those goals (Tileston, 2004).

Relevance, high interest, choice, and authenticity are crucial criteria in motivating young adolescents (Beamon, 2001).

School-to-career initiatives allow students to successfully transition to the real world of work because they make school experiences relevant (Thiers, 1995).

HOW: CLASSROOM APPLICATION

- Open your lesson by telling students what they will be taught and why they need to know it. If you relate content to students' personal lives, students have a reason for paying attention to the lesson.

- Whenever the opportunity presents itself, use real-life examples to illustrate a point that you are teaching. Connecting course content to real-life examples motivates students and increases interest.

- Engaging students in real-life projects not only ensures that content will be remembered but enables you to consolidate and teach a large numbers of objectives simultaneously. For example, have students create a Civil War newspaper as a project. Work with students to create a rubric that will be used to assess the newspaper. Each newspaper may include a title, a byline, a table of contents, a feature story with an image, an editorial, an ad, and a crime report. Not only will students demonstrate their comprehension of the Civil War but they will also learn the function of the parts of a newspaper.

- Take students on a field trip to a location that connects the content being taught to the real world. Teachers often wait too late to take the field trip. Taking that trip earlier will make the learning more relevant and provide students with a real-world connection to the content. I still remember taking a field trip to the Young People's Concert, which the Atlanta Symphony sponsored when I was in elementary school. This annual event is one of the reasons that I still possess a love for all different types of music.

- Work-study not only reduces behavioral infractions but also makes content extremely relevant to all brains. For example, when students are placed in alternative education due to their inability to be successful in a regular school setting, they are often involved in work-study or on-the-job training. Career academies and High Schools That Work programs also take advantage of the fact that students learn to do real jobs by doing real jobs. Apprenticeships, internships, practica, and student teaching are all viable and effective ways to help students comprehend and retain knowledge and skill. Assign students to experts in a field who can involve them in a work-study experience related to course content. Then step back and watch them learn!

- Invite guest speakers who are experts in a field of interest to students to come and address the class regarding their profession. Motivating speakers often increase students' knowledge of a particular field of study and may encourage them to pursue the field as a future profession.

REFLECTION

What is my plan for making the learning relevant in my classroom?

Objective/Standard: _____

_____

_____

_____

Connection to Real Life: _____

_____

_____

_____

Objective/Standard: _____

_____

_____

_____

Connection to Real Life: _____

_____

_____

_____

Objective/Standard: _____

_____

_____

_____

Connection to Real Life: _____

_____

_____

_____

Objective/Standard: _____

_____

_____

_____

Connection to Real Life: _____

_____

_____

_____

<h1>Strategy 10</h1>

<h1>Focusing the Brain</h1>

Marcia L. Tate

WHAT: DEFINING THE STRATEGY

Whether referred to as concept, mind, or semantic maps or as word webs or graphic organizers, these tools are some of the best friends of a teacher who desires to facilitate the comprehension of students. They address both the left and the right hemispheres of students, so they are beneficial to all. The students strong in left hemisphere can supply the verbage, and the right-hemisphere students have the option of showing what they know pictorially. Have students draw the organizer along with you as you explain the major concepts and details.

When I teach my class *Worksheets Don't Grow Dendrites*, a picture of a neuron serves as a graphic organizer or mind map for the five elements of a brain-compatible classroom. The main ideas are in boxes and the details are written underneath. Main ideas and details are color-coded. See the diagram below. By the time I have finished teaching this part of the class, teachers know that the best classrooms are ones where students are actively engaged in the learning—talking to one another, moving to learn content, connecting ideas together, thinking positively, and having a purpose for the learning.

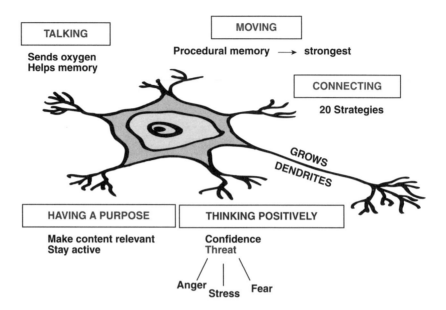

WHY: THEORETICAL FRAMEWORK

Graphic organizers are effective tools for supporting thinking and learning in four major ways: (1) abstract information is represented in a concrete format, (2) relationships between facts and concepts are depicted, (3) new information is connected to previous knowledge, and (4) thoughts are organized for writing and for problem solving. (Ronis, 2006)

Graphic organizers, scaffolding, and activating prior knowledge are techniques that are research proven to help teachers better connect with students. (Deshler & Schumaker, 2006)

Graphic organizers represent a form of nonlinguistic representation and are one of the most popular ways teachers can have students represent the knowledge that they have experienced. (Marzano, 2007, p. 52)

The models and mental maps that students produce prior to a unit of study enable teachers to correct misunderstandings and expand on their prior knowledge. (Jensen, 2007)

Mind mapping, a very special form of imagery, combines pictures with language to assist students in seeing how concepts are related to other concepts and how they connect to a main idea. (Sousa, 2006)

Having students create a mind or concept map is a meaningful strategy for helping them make sense of and learn vast amounts of new content. (Budd, 2004)

Graphic organizers not only gain the attention of students but can also improve comprehension, meaning, and retention. (Sousa, 2007)

Frustration can be avoided when teachers allow students to structure their ideas into the easily understood format that an original mind map can provide. (Goldberg, 2004)

Because the brain remembers images more easily than just words, graphic organizers are one of the tools that are effective for organizing patterns. (Feinstein, 2004)

Graphic organizers enable English learners to organize words and ideas in a way that helps them see patterns and relationships in mathematics. (Coggins, Kravin, Coates, & Carrol, 2007)

Concept maps, a type of graphic organizer, integrate both visual and verbal activities and enhance comprehension of concrete, abstract, verbal, and nonverbal concepts. (Sousa, 2006)

Graphic organizers are powerful tools for instruction since they enable students to organize data into segments or chunks that they can comprehend and manage. (Gregory & Parry, 2006, p. 198)

Flow charts, continuums, matrices, Venn diagrams, concept maps, and problem-solution charts are all types of graphic representations that can be used by mathematics teachers because they can be quickly understood and can provide structure for synthesizing new information. (Posamentier & Jaye, 2006)

When graphic organizers are used to change words into images, both left- and right-brain learners can use those images to see the big picture. (Gregory & Parry, 2006)

HOW: INSTRUCTIONAL ACTIVITIES

WHO: Elementary/Middle/High
WHEN: Before and after the lesson
CONTENT AREA(S): All

• To access students' prior knowledge and summarize content after a lesson is taught, have students complete a K-N-L graphic organizer. Have students discuss or brainstorm (1) what they already *know* about a concept or unit of study; (2) what they will *need* to know to comprehend the concept, and (3) following instruction, what they have *learned*.

K-N-L Graphic Organizer		
Topic:		
What I Know	*What I Need to Know*	*What I Learned*

WHO: Elementary/Middle/High
WHEN: During the lesson
CONTENT AREA(S):   All

- Because the brain thinks in chunks or connections, have students increase their knowledge of vocabulary by using a word web. As new vocabulary is introduced, have students complete the word web below by brainstorming additional synonyms for the new word. Students can keep their word webs in a notebook for review and add synonyms throughout the year. Encourage them to add these words to their speaking and writing vocabularies as well.

Word Web

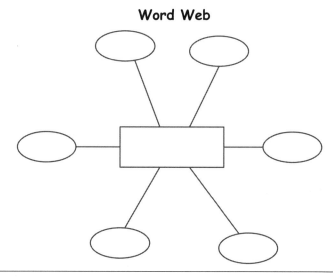

WHO: Elementary/Middle/High
WHEN: After the lesson
CONTENT AREA(S):   All

- After the reading of a story or novel where problems exist that must be resolved, have students complete the following story frame to demonstrate their understanding of the story's plot.

Story Map

Title: _____

Setting:

Characters: _____   _____
_____   _____
_____   _____

Problem:

Event 1 _____
Event 2 _____
Event 3 _____
Event 4 _____

Solution:

WHO: Elementary/Middle/High
WHEN: During the lesson
CONTENT AREA(S):   All

- To help students identify the main idea and details in narrative or content-area texts, have them complete the following graphic organizer. It will assist students in understanding that supporting details should add up to the main idea.

Main Idea/Details

Details

Main Idea

WHO: Elementary/Middle/High
WHEN: During the lesson
CONTENT AREA(S):   All

• Have students identify cause-effect relationships in narrative and content-area texts by completing the graphic organizer below. This will help them understand that every action has an accompanying effect.

Cause/Effect

So

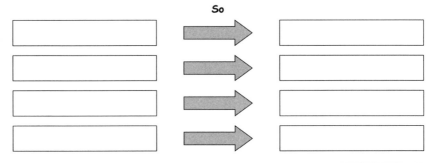

WHO: Elementary/Middle/High
WHEN: During the lesson
CONTENT AREA(S):   All

• Have students complete the following graphic organizer to demonstrate their understanding of a character's traits and to site evidence in narrative or expository texts to support the given traits.

Character Traits

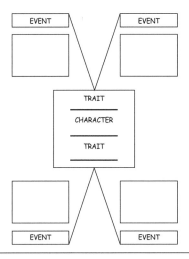

WHO: Elementary/Middle/High
WHEN: During the lesson
CONTENT AREA(S): All

- Have students complete the following graphic organizer to identify sequence of events and to show how one event leads to another in either narrative or content-area texts.

Sequence

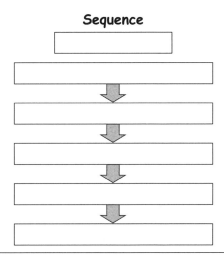

WHO: Elementary/Middle/High
WHEN: During the lesson
CONTENT AREA(S):   All

• Have students compare and contrast two or more characters or events in narrative or content-area texts by using the following Venn diagram.

Compare/Contrast

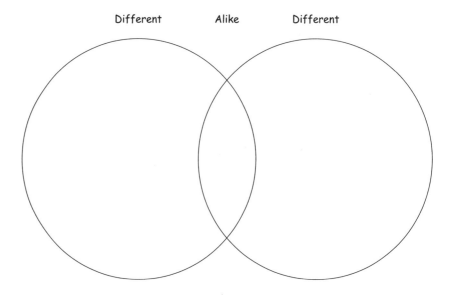

Different   Alike   Different

WHO: Elementary/Middle/High
WHEN: During the lesson
CONTENT AREA(S):   All

• While lecturing or discussing ideas with students, complete a semantic, concept, or mind map on the board to show how the major concepts are related to one another. Have students copy the map in their notes as you explain each part. See a sample format below.

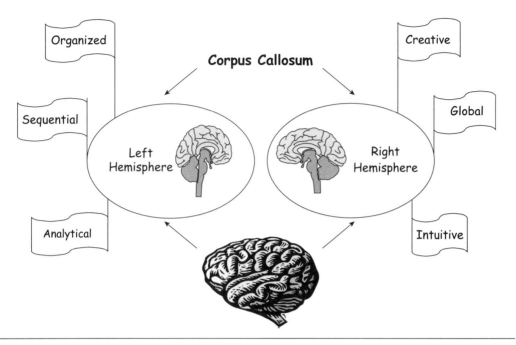

Organized

Creative

Corpus Callosum

Sequential

Global

Left Hemisphere

Right Hemisphere

Analytical

Intuitive

WHO: Elementary/Middle/High
WHEN: After the lesson
CONCEPT AREA(S): All

- Once you have demonstrated how to do so, encourage students to create their own semantic, concept, or mind maps regarding a unit of study. This technique alone will enhance comprehension because these mind maps can be reviewed prior to testing to facilitate long-term retention.

WHO: Elementary/Middle
WHEN: Before, during, and after the lesson
CONCEPT AREA(S): All

- Refer to the series *Engage the Brain: Graphic Organizers and Other Visual Strategies* to find additional graphic organizers in the content areas of language arts, math, science, and social studies. Grades K–5 have all content areas contained in the same book. Grades 6–8 have separate books for each of the four content areas. Consult the Corwin website at www.corwin.com for information.

REFLECTION AND APPLICATION

> How will I incorporate *graphic organizers* into instruction to engage students' brains?

Standard/Objective: _____

_____

Activity: _____

_____

Standard/Objective: _____

_____

Activity: _____

_____

Standard/Objective: _____

_____

Activity: _____

_____

Standard/Objective: _____

_____

Activity: _____

_____

Standard/Objective: _____

_____

Activity: _____

_____

Standard/Objective: _____

_____

Activity: _____

_____

Energizing
the Brain

Eric Jensen

Chapter Preview

◆ **The Sweet Sounds of Learning**
  • **Music's Role in the Classroom**
◆ **Energizing Your Classroom**
  • **Using Energizers With Your Students**

Ups and downs plague the human brain. We awaken, we're groggy, we're active, we get sleepy after lunch, and then we're active again. Just after dinner, we feel sleepy again. Our internal clock regulates our sleep, activity, and cycles, which would never be an issue except that school time requires so much attention. Students would love to take more naps during the day, but we're expected to keep them focused enough to concentrate. That's a challenge unless you have some practical and proven strategies. This chapter is about getting and keeping students active. Music and energizers are both premier tools for raising student energy.

THE SWEET SOUNDS OF LEARNING

Results show that music affects the emotions, respiratory system, heart rate, posture, and mental images of the listener. These effects can dramatically alter the composite mood, state, and physiology of a person. As you change the state of your students, you get direct access to behavioral changes. Music works marvelously to energize, align groups, induce relaxation, stimulate prior experiences, develop rapport, set the theme or the tone for the day, stimulate the mind, facilitate fun, and inspire.

Does music belong in a classroom where the subject is not music? Absolutely! And there are many ways to use it. Chances are, you learned the letters of the alphabet with a song. You probably learned many words and phrases through folk songs. You learned rituals, manners, and social skills with childhood songs. As you've gotten older, you have associated many situations, feelings, and people with special songs. This is because listening to and playing music is a powerful way to learn.

FIGURE 11.1   Advantages of using music in the classroom

- Embeds the learning faster, on a deeper level, like the "Alphabet Song"
- Provides relaxation after stress or discouragement
- Collects and brings the whole group together
- Motivates the group to get up and get going
- Builds rapport and encourages bonding
- Energizes and brings new life to the group
- Appeals to the particular cultural values of the group
- Comforts the soul during painful times
- Lets students have fun when they need a change of mind-set
- Boosts achievement by activating the thinking portion of the brain
- Harmonizes situations when the group seems to be on edge
- Calms down hyper students
- Stimulates the right-brain hemisphere, activating more of the brain
- Increases attentiveness and concentration
- Stimulates and focuses creativity
- Takes some pressure off the teacher
- Creates sound curtains to isolate classes or groups from distracting noise

---

Music's Role in the Classroom

Kids relate to music. And most classrooms do not use music as an integral or emotional learning tool. The first thing most kids (and many adults) do when they get out of class, get in a car, or arrive home is listen to music to relax, energize, change moods, feel good. So, why don't schools incorporate it more? We decorate the walls visually; why not appeal to and utilize the other senses, such as auditory and kinesthetic? To make your learning environment much more student friendly and build rapport with kids, enhance the learning process with music.

How to Use Music

No one needs to tell you your favorite songs. Here, we'll walk through some smart rules for using music. Many questioning techniques go through my head when I decide which music to play:

- What's the task/activity that's coming up?
- What's the optimal emotional/physical reaction I need from students (e.g., calm, energized, silly, focused, relaxed)?

◆ Will students need to talk during the task? (Use instrumental pieces during concentrated, quiet work and vocalized music for group work.)
◆ What are the primary cultures in my classroom?
◆ What are the music and movies of my students' generation?
◆ Which music selection will likely accomplish my task?

First and foremost, all music has some sort of pace. When selecting music for the classroom, consider its tempo (i.e., beats per minute). The beat of the music affects both heart rate and breathing—the two most important determiners of mood, feelings, and state. In general, your selections should be instrumental. Exceptions will include some popular music, but these may be reserved for breaks or special events outside of lecture time (e.g., birthdays, celebrations, a quick reward for a job well done).

Learning to maximize the use of music in the classroom is an ongoing process. Match the specific music to the teachable task. Prepare ahead of time so you're calmer in the moment when you use the music. Here is an example of types of music that you could use:

◆ baroque/classical (for seat work, discussion time)
◆ callbacks (classic songs for coming back to the classroom after recess, a fire drill, or lunch or just to start the day)
◆ classic R&B (for fun sing-along)
◆ classic rock (gets things done fast)
◆ closing/good-bye (send them home with these)
◆ high-tempo vocals (current pop songs for activities with no talking needed)
◆ high-tempo instrumental (fast for movement)
◆ mellow New Age (to play in the background during seatwork)
◆ upbeat New Age (for focused, conversational work)
◆ oldies (for sing-alongs, and to get things done)
◆ slow instrumental (for stretching, to wake up the body)
◆ themes from TV shows (such as the Mission Impossible theme for a challenging assignment or the Jeopardy theme for a student-organized quiz show)
◆ world music (for transition, cultural studies)

Use music as a partner and an aid in the learning process. Always be sensitive to the existing mood in the classroom, and respect it. Music can increase students' energy level, match their existing level, or bring it down. If a sensitive, troubling, or emotional process just took place, avoid music or use low-volume, low-key music that matches the mood. If a high-energy activity just took place, be ready with upbeat, high-energy music to match the mood. Music should serenade and invite students (and maybe provide an occasional nudge). It should never intrude.

How Much Music Is Ideal?

Assuming that you are not a music teacher (in which case, music would be the focus), use music sparingly. The more you use it, the more likely students are to habituate to it. They'll get tired of your songs and start ignoring you. Be strategic. In any given hour, I might have music on for 10 to 30 percent of the time. The selections I use the most are instrumentals that play during seatwork. If you find yourself flustered and caught off guard by not having your next music selection ready, that's a sign. You might be talking or lecturing too much. Remember, more of them, less of you. When students are working independently, with partners, or in small groups, use the time to plan the next piece of music.

Practical Solutions for Using Music

Be sensitive to the needs of your students. Tell them that you will use music to enhance their learning. Turn the volume up or down slowly when you use it. This makes it easier on the ears. As with addressing the eye's sensitivity to bright light, it is less shocking to your students' ears if you introduce sounds gradually.

Be flexible and listen to your students. If they want to bring their own music, set two requirements. First, you have to preview it to ensure that it is compatible with the messages and values of your classroom. Second, you decide when and how to use it. Take advantage of the Internet; you can Google the name of the song, along with the word lyrics, and get the lyrics in seconds. If you don't like the music, don't play it—but tell the student who suggested it that you appreciate the suggestion, and ask for other choices. The key is to maintain your relationship with your students; use music as a bridge, not as a way to emphasize differences in taste. Have fun with it. Music is a great team builder.

If a learner complains, the volume may be too high; turn it down a bit and make sure that person can see you do so. The student may be an auditory learner; if so, move his or her seat position farther away from the music. Or the student may simply need time to adjust. Be sure to acknowledge and respect the various needs of your students, and thank them for their input. And make sure that you explain more about the music—why you use it and how it can assist learning. Always make it clear that learners can switch seats at any time.

ENERGIZING YOUR CLASSROOM

Energizers are short, simple, high-energy activities. They can be done individually, with a partner, in a small group, as a team, or as a class. One of the many benefits of energizers is that they can help us remember things better. How? Quick physical activity boosts the "uppers" in the body, including norepinephrine and epinephrine, both of which are memory fixatives. In addition, the body stores glucose (as glycogen) in the liver, and physical activity triggers the release of glycogen. That's important because enhanced (but not too high) levels of glucose support memory formation. For energizers to work, they have to be well thought out, set up right, followed through, and spaced out well. Consider these questions: What was the last energizer you did? How did that go over?

An energizer is just a framework for movement. There is no such thing as a bad energizer for your students, but make sure the energizers are age appropriate. For example, you take an elementary-level energizer and upgrade it for adults. There's always a way to add an element, speed it up, slow it down, or add variety to it. If you run out of ideas for energizers, get help from your students, who can work in teams or groups to come up with one energizer per week.

Be sure to keep in mind that some of your students will have special needs. Kids with attention deficit disorder, learning delays, auditory processing issues, or sensory issues will have a tough time with directions unless you post them visually and keep them simple. Use gestures, but remember to do so one at a time. Kids with Asperger syndrome, for example, will have great difficulties with activities that require social processing (reading faces and intent in others). Remember to think through each activity to ensure that it will work for all your students. If it won't, modify it or give some students special assignments so that they can be included in other ways.

Using Energizers With Your Students

Provide a variety of energizers for the whole class. If space is a precious commodity, offer "stand in place" energizers or ones for sitting. Never decide against using an energizer if it's needed; just modify it (e.g., tone it down, make it shorter). Your students will continue to learn if they're in a good learning state. Otherwise, boredom and tiredness are two terrible enemies in the pursuit of knowledge.

Giving the Right Directions

Most of us were never taught how to give directions. We just assume we know how. So we often create states of confusion, resistance, or apathy when we really need states of motivation. To give flawless directions, every time, use this formula:

1. Use a set-up to engage—it's the why.

2. Give a specific start time—it's the when.

3. Use a consistent trigger word or action—it's the starter for when.

4. Give the directions one at a time—they're the what and how.

5. Check students' readiness to take action—it's your insurance that it'll work.

6. Give the same trigger word—it's the when again.

Now, let's flesh out the details of these steps. The first step is to use a set-up to frame the energizer. This is your brief transition to the energizer from what you were doing before. Do not assume that everyone is ready to jump. Effectively setting things up helps your students immediately get why they are about to do something different. To a first grader, you might say, "Ooh! I just thought of a great idea!" All of the kids' heads will turn to you and look up—what is the great idea?! To a class of high school students, you'd need a different angle. Raise your own hand and ask the class, "How many of you would like something totally off the wall as a break from studying? Great. The ____ team is up next with their quick energizer for us." With adults, you might say, "How many of you have noticed that your chair is not very ergonomic? Postural stress can get us all a bit cranky, so let's take a quick stretch."

The second step is to give a specific start time for the energizer. This is critical because if you don't, and instead go right into the directions, some students will get out of their seats and start following them while you're still talking (so they can get a head start). This is disruptive, and they may not even have the directions right. The start time alerts them to the forthcoming event. You might begin by saying, "In just 10 seconds . . ." (never less than 10 or more than 30; it has to do with our perception of urgency). You want your students to pay attention because the event is coming up fast.

The third step is to give a consistent trigger word or action such as "When I say 'Go!' . . ." or "When the music starts. . . ." This creates a mental cue and primes students' brains for that one word or event. Use the same word or phrase consistently so that you never need to try to recall what your trigger word was.

The fourth step is to begin giving the directions, but only one at a time. Almost all directions have multiple steps, but resist the temptation to give them all at once. If your students are already standing, you might say, "Please take 10 giant steps in any direction." Notice that this gives them choice—that's a good idea. They're more likely to do something if they can do it their way. But what happens if they each end up with their best friend? If you think this might compromise the activity, remedy it, but not by lecturing them. Say, "Hey, how did so many of you end up with your best friends?" And add another short step. Say, "Great! Now please stand back to back with your neighbor and take seven new steps." This will disburse them all in a new direction with no reprimand from you.

Although I've just told you to give directions in small chunks, just one at a time, there are plenty of exceptions. In some cases, students may need to work at their own pace. In other cases, there may be complex directions and it's too disruptive to stop start, stop, and start again. To solve that problem, you'll need to post the directions. Use a flip chart, a white board, or a slide to list all the directions so that everyone can see them and proceed through the task without your constant explanation.

The fifth step is critical. Even with the best of plans, things can fall flat. So you need to check students' readiness to take action. As a generalization, there are three common emotional states that your students will experience after you announce the first direction and before you tell them to "go." These are the ABCs of state readiness:

A is for anticipation: Students lean forward, hands on knees—meaning they are good to go. If you see this state in nearly all of your students, they are ready for the next step: the trigger word.

B is for backing off: Apathetic signs include leaning back in their chairs and rolling their eyes—meaning they are not buying into what you're asking them to do. Increase their buy-in by improving your framing of the event. Give them a better reason to do what you're asking them to do.

C is for confusion: They look side to side for help from peers, and their foreheads may be wrinkled—meaning they don't understand what you're asking them to do. Offer directions again, and either simplify them, review them, or say them differently.

Finally we get to the sixth and last of our direction-giving steps. Give the trigger word you introduced earlier. Be consistent with it, and say it with enthusiasm, with your hands matching the nonverbal communications, "Ready, set . . . go!"

Suggestions for Energizers

The Ball Toss. Five to seven students stand in a circle about 7 to 10 feet apart, facing each other. One has a ball (e.g., a wad of paper, a beanbag). He or she tosses it to another student to start the game. Content could be any number of things, including Q&A, continuing a story, giving a compliment, word association, math facts, and geography. Keep the game fast and light. Give students control with clear rules: (1) call the other person's name, and make eye contact before passing the ball; (2) pass the ball higher than his or her head; and (3) never pass to the person on your right or left, only someone across from you.

Clap Happy. You start a clap or a rhythm, and students pass it around the room. After yours makes it through the whole group, the first student starts a new one, and others follow suit. Students listen and repeat the patterns. This is good for memory and music skills.

Follow the Leader. A group leader stands. He or she leads, and the rest of the group mirrors his or her actions. The leader can act, dance, stretch, walk, jog, or wiggle, and the others follow along.

Simon Says. All stand and do only what Simon (i.e., you) says to do. Give instructions to follow, some of them prefaced with "Simon says" and others without. Go at a moderate pace. If students make a mistake, they keep playing. Always make it a win for all, so no one's ever out of the game. There are many variations. You can use it as: a listening game, for following instructions; a get-to-know-you game, pointing to or saying or facing a name you call out; a geography game ("Simon Says point to the direction of . . . "); a math game ("Simon says use your body to give me the answer to $5 + 6 = $ . . . "); a language-learning game ("Simon says point to su boca or su mano); a science game ("Simon says point to something in this room made of steel/made of glass/made of plastic/that's over 20 years old/that would not have existed 50 years ago").

Touch 'n' Go. Have students get up and, in sequence, touch five pieces of metal, four pieces of glass, three of wood, two of leather, one of plastic or rubber. All items must be at least 10 or more feet apart. Provide variations with the content: math—touch right angles, cylinders, cubes, rectangles, length, height; science—touch textures, colors, weights, rarity, solids; history—touch things that fit a certain time era; English—touch objects that could be used to make a sentence, that have double meanings, that are capitalized; economics—touch items in order of value, cost. Once all items have been touched, students sit down.

SUMMARY

All of us know the critical importance of managing students' emotional states. There are countless ways to do it, and this chapter focuses on two of them: music and energizers. When using music, it is key to consider the following: What's the task/activity that's coming up? What's the optimal emotional/physical reaction you need from students? Will students need to talk during the task? What are the primary cultures in your classroom? What are the music and movies of your students' generation? Which music selection will likely accomplish your task?

Keeping students engaged while sitting for extended periods of time is a challenge. For this reason, energizers are crucial. So get them up and moving! Keep in mind that good directions are often the difference between an activity working and an activity falling flat, and learn fewer energizers well (and know how to vary them) instead of trying to learn countless ones. Then you won't be stuck with tired, slumped, bored students. Energize their bodies and brains with music and activities.

Reflection

◆ What are your feelings about the topics presented in this chapter?

◆ What are some practical applications for what you're learning?

◆ What do you want to remember from this chapter?

References

Chapter 1

Arbib, M. A. (2005). From monkey-like action recognition to human language: An evolutionary framework for neurolinguistics. *The Behavioral and Brain Sciences, 2,* 105–124.

Balu, D. T., & Lucki, I. (2009, March). Adult hippocampal neurogenesis: Regulation, functional implications, and contribution to disease pathology. *Neuroscience & Biobehavioral Reviews, 33,* 232–252.

Bateman, B., Warner, J. O., Hutchinson, E., Dean, T., Rowlandson, P., Gant, C., . . . Stevenson, J. (2004). The effects of a double blind, placebo controlled artificial food colorings and benzoate preservative challenge on hyperactivity in a general population sample of preschool children. *Archives of Diseases in Childhood, 89,* 506–511.

Bauerlein, M. (2011). Too dumb for complex texts? *Educational Leadership, 68,* 28–32.

Beatty, J. (2001). *The human brain: Essentials of behavioral neuroscience.* Thousand Oaks, CA: Sage.

Brannon, E. M., & van der Walle, G. (2001). Ordinal numerical knowledge in young children. *Cognitive Psychology, 43,* 53–81.

Butterworth, B. (1999). *What counts: How every brain is hardwired for math.* New York: Free Press.

Centers for Disease Control and Prevention. (2010). *U.S. obesity trends.* Available online at www.cdc.gov

Dehaene, S. (2010). The calculating brain. In D. A. Sousa (Ed.), *Mind, brain, & education: Neuroscience implications for the classroom* (pp. 179–198). Bloomington, IN: Solution Tree Press.

Deng, W., Aimone, J. B., & Gage, F. H. (2010). New neurons and new memories: How does adult hippocampal neurogenesis affect learning and memory? *Nature Reviews Neuroscience, 11*(5), 339–350.

Devlin, K. (2000). *The math gene: How mathematical thinking evolved and why numbers are like gossip.* New York: Basic Books.

Diamond, J. (1992). *The third chimpanzee: The evolution and future of the human animal.* New York: Harper Perennial.

Diamond, M., & Hopson, J. (1998). *Magic trees of the mind: How to nurture your child's intelligence, creativity, and healthy emotions from birth through adolescence.* New York: Dutton.

Dosenbach, N. U., Nardos, B., Cohen, A. L., Fair, D. A., Power, J. D., Church, J. A., . . . Schlaggar, B. L. (2010). Prediction of individual brain maturity using fMRI. *Science, 329,* 1358–1361.

Gazzaniga, M. S., Ivry, R. B., & Mangun, G. R. (2002). *Cognitive neuroscience: The biology of the mind* (2nd ed.). New York: Norton.

Geday, J., & Gjedde, A. (2009). Attention, emotion, and deactivation of default activity in inferior medial prefrontal cortex. *Brain and Cognition, 69,* 344–352.

Goldberg, E. (2001). *The executive brain: Frontal lobes and the civilized mind.* New York: Oxford.

Grall, T. (2009). *Custodial mothers and fathers and their child support: 2007.* Washington, DC: U.S. Census Bureau.

Kitamura, T., Mishina, M., & Sugiyama, H. (2006). Dietary restriction increases hippocampal neurogenesis by molecular mechanisms independent of NMDA receptors. *Neuroscience Letters, 393*(2–3), 94–96.

Korol, D. L., & Gold, P. E. (1998). Glucose, memory, and aging. *American Journal of Clinical Nutrition, 67,* 764S–771S.

Lieberman, B. (2005). Study narrows search for brain's memory site. *Brain in the News, 12,* 4.

Luciana, M., Conklin, H. M., Hooper, C. J., & Yarger, R. S. (2005). The development of nonverbal working memory and executive control processes in adolescents. *Child Development, 76,* 697–712.

MacLean, P. D., *The triune brain in evolution: Role in paleocerebral functions.* New York: Plenum Press.

Medina, J. (2008). *Brain rules.* Seattle, WA: Pear Press.

Meerlo, P., Mistlberger, R. E., Jacobs, B. L., Heller, H. C., & McGinty, D. (2009). New neurons in the adult brain: The role of sleep and the consequences of sleep loss. *Sleep Medicine Reviews, 13,* 187–194.

Millichap, J. G., & Yee, M. M. (2003). The diet factor in pediatric and adolescent migraine. *Pediatric Neurology, 28,* 9–15.

Monk, C. A., Trafton, J. G., & Boehm-Davis, D. A. (2008). The effect of interruption duration and demand on resuming suspended goals. *Journal of Experimental Psychology: Applied, 14*(4), 299–313.

National Governors Association. (2005). *2005 Rate Your Future Survey.* Washington, DC: Author. Available online at http://www.nga.org

Oberman, L. M., Hubbard, E. M., McCleery, J. P., Altschuler, E. L., Ramachandran, V. S., & Pineda, J. A. (2005). EEG evidence for mirror neuron dysfunction in autism spectrum disorders. *Cognitive Brain Research, 24,* 190–198.

Pancsofar, N., & Vernon-Feagans, L. (2006). Mother and father language input to young children: Contributions to later language development. *Journal of Applied Developmental Psychology, 27,* 571–587.

Paus, T. (2005). Mapping brain maturation and cognitive development during adolescence. *Trends in Cognitive Sciences, 9,* 60–68.

Pereira, A. C., Huddleston, D. E., Brickman, A. M., Sosunov, A. A., Hen, R., McKhann, G. M., . . . Small, S. A. (2007). An in vivo correlate of exercise-induced neurogenesis in the adult dentate gyrus. *Proceedings of the National Academy of Sciences USA, 104,* 5638–5643.

Pulvermüller, F. (2010). Brain embodiment of syntax and grammar: Discrete combinatorial mechanisms spelt out in neuronal circuits. *Brain and Language, 112,* 167–179.

Reiss, D., Neiderheiser, J., Hetherington, E. M., & Plomin, R. (2000). *The relationship code: Deciphering genetic and social influences on adolescent development.* Cambridge, MA: Harvard University Press.

Restak, R. M. (2001). *The secret life of the brain.* Washington, DC: Dana Press.

Rideout, V. J., Foehr, U. G., & Roberts, D. F. (2010). *Generation M2: Media in the lives of 8- to 18-year-olds.* Menlo Park, CA: Kaiser Family Foundation.

Smith, M. A., Riby, L. M., van Eekelen, J., & Foster, J. K. (2011). Glucose enhancement of human memory: A comprehensive research review of the glucose memory facilitation effect. *Neuroscience & Biobehavioral Reviews, 35,* 770–783.

Squire, L. R., & Kandel, E. R. (1999). *Memory: From mind to molecules.* New York: W. H. Freeman.

Steinberg, L. (2005). Cognitive and effective development in adolescence. *Trends in Cognitive Sciences, 9,* 69–74.

Sünram-Lea, S. I., Dewhurst, S. A., & Foster, J. K. (2008). The effect of glucose administration on the recollection and familiarity components of recognition memory. *Biological Psychology, 77,* 69–75.

Taras, H. (2005). Physical activity and student performance at school. *Journal of School Health, 75,* 214–218.

Yazzie-Mintz, E. (2010). *Charting the path from engagement to achievement: A report on the 2009 High School Survey of Student Engagement.* Bloomington, IN: Center for Evaluation and Education Policy.

Chapter 2

Ramachandran, V. S. (2006). Mirror neurons and the brain in a vat. *Edge: The Third Culture.* Retrieved May 6, 2010, from http://www.edge.org/3rd_culture/ramachandran06/ramachandran06_index.html.

Ratey, J. (with Hagerman, E.). (2008). *Spark: The revolutionary new science of exercise and the brain.* New York: Little, Brown and Company.

Rizzolatti, G., & Sinigaglia, C. (2007). *Mirrors in the brain: How our minds share actions and emotions.* Oxford, UK: Oxford University Press.

Chapter 3

Angelo, T., & Cross, K. P. (1998). *Classroom assessment techniques: A handbook for college teachers* (2nd ed.). San Francisco: Jossey-Bass.

Bangert-Drowns, R., Kulik, C. C., Kulik, J. A., & Morgan, M. (1991). The instructional effect of feedback in test-like events. *Review of Educational Research, 61*(2), 213–238.

Bloom, F. E., Beal, M. F., & Kupfer, D. J. (Eds.). (2006). *The Dana guide to brain health.* Available from www.dana.org

Carney, R. N., & Levin, J. R. (2000). Mnemonic instruction, with a focus on transfer. *Journal of Educational Psychology, 92*(4), 783–790.

Elkind, D. (1978). Understanding the young adolescent. *Adolescence, 13,* 127–134.

Epstein, H. T. (2001). *An outline of the role of brain in human cognitive development. Brain and Cognition, 45*(1), 44–51.

Giedd, J., Blumenthal, J., Jeffries, N. O., Castellanos, F., Liu, H., Zijdenbos, A., et al. (1999). Brain development during childhood and adolescence: A longitudinal MRI study. *Nature Neuroscience, 2*(10), 861–863.

Giedd, J. N., Castellanos, F. X., Rajapakse, J. C., Vaituzis, A. C., & Rapoport, J. L. (1997). Sexual dimorphism of the developing human brain. *Progress in Neuro-Psychopharmacology & Biological Psychiatry, 21*(8), 1185–1201.

Koepp, M. J., Gunn, R. N., Lawrence, A. D., Cunningham, V. J., Dagher, A., Jones, T., et al. (1998, May 21). Evidence for striatal dopamine release during a video game. *Nature, 393*(6682), 266–268.

Marzano, R., Pickering, D., & Pollock, J. (2001). *Classroom instruction that works: Research-based strategies for increasing student achievement.* Alexandria, VA: Association for Supervision and Curriculum Development.

Mason, M. (1998). *The van Hiele levels of geometric understanding.* Retrieved April 26, 2009, from www.coe.tamu.edu/~rcapraro/Graduate_Courses/EDCI%20 624% 20625/EDCI%20624%20CD/literature/van%20Hiele%20Levels.pdf

Neimark, E. D. (1975). Intellectual development during adolescence. In F. D. Horowitz (Ed.), *Review of child development research* (Vol. 4, pp. 541–594). Chicago: University of Chicago Press.

Raz, N., Gunning-Dixon, F., Head, D., Williamson, A., & Acker, J. D. (2001). Age and sex differences in the cerebellum and ventral pons: A prospective MR study of healthy adults. *American Journal of Neuroradiology, 22*(6), 1161–1167.

Schneider, B. H., & Younger, A. J. (1996). Adolescent-parent attachment and adolescents' relations with their peers. *Youth and Society, 28*(1), 95–108.

Sousa, D. A. (2003). *How the gifted brain learns.* Thousand Oaks, CA: Corwin.

Spear, L. P. (2000). The adolescent brain and age-related behavioral manifestations. *Neuroscience and Biobehavioral Reviews, 24*(4), 417–463.

Wang, A., & Thomas, M. (1995). Effects of keywords on long-term retention: Help or hindrance? *Journal of Educational Psychology, 87,* 468–475.

Chapter 4

Allen, J. (2009, March 19–21). *Real kids, real books, real reading, real results.* Presentation given at the Illinois Reading Council Conference, Reading! Engage! Excite! Ignite! Springfield, IL.

Bell, N. (1991). *Visualizing and verbalizing for language comprehension and thinking.* San Luis Obispo, CA: Gander.

Carter, R. (1998). *Mapping the mind.* Berkeley: University of California Press.

Joshi, R. M., Treiman, R, Carreker, S., & Moats, L. C. (2009). How words cast their spell: Spelling is an integral part of learning the language, not a matter of memorization. *American Educator, 32*(4), 6–16, 42.

Juel, C., & Deffes, R. (2004). Making words stick: What research says about reading. *Educational Leadership, 61,* 30–34.

Keller, T. A., & Just, M. A. (2009, December 10). Altering cortical connectivity: Remediation-induced changes in the white matter of poor readers. *Neuron.* Retrieved July 21, 2010, from http://www.psy.cmu.edu/news/news_2009_12_10.pdf.

McCollough, A. W., & Vogel, E. K. (2008). Your inner spam filter: What makes you so smart? Might be your lizard brain. *Scientific American Mind, 19*(3), 74–77.

Nevills, P., & Wolfe, P. (2009). *Building the reading brain* (2nd ed.). Thousand Oaks, CA: Corwin.

Nolte, J. (2002). *The human brain: An introduction to its functional anatomy* (5th ed.). St. Louis, MO: Mosby.

Poldrack, R. A., & Rodriguez, P. (2004). How do memory systems interact? Evidence from human classification and learning. *Neurobiology of Learning and Memory, 82,* 324–332.

Shaywitz, S. (2003). *Overcoming dyslexia: A new and complete science-based program for reading problems at any level.* New York: Alfred A. Knopf.

Sylwester, R. (2005). *How to explain a brain: An educator's handbook of brain terms and cognitive processes.* Thousand Oaks, CA: Corwin.

Chapter 5

Ashcraft, M. H. (1995). Cognitive psychology and simple arithmetic: A review and summary of new directions. *Mathematical Cognition, 1,* 3–34.

Brannon, E. M. (2005, March). The independence of language and mathematical reasoning. *Proceedings of the National Academy of Sciences, 102,* 3177–3178.

Dehaene, S. (1997). *The number sense: How the mind creates mathematics.* New York: Oxford University Press.

Dehaene, S., Spelke, E., Pinel, P., Stanescu, R., & Tsivkin, S. (1999, May). Sources of mathematical thinking: Behavioral and brain-imaging evidence. *Science, 284,* 970–974.

Devlin, K. (2000). *The math gene: How mathematical thinking evolved and why numbers are like gossip.* New York: Basic Books.

Griffin, S. (2002). The development of math competence in the preschool and early school years: Cognitive foundations and instructional strategies. In J. M. Rover (Ed.). *Mathematical cognition: A volume in current perspectives on cognition, learning, and instruction* (pp. 1–32). Greenwich, CT: Information Age Publishing.

Ischebeck, A., Zamarian, L., Siedentopf, C., Koppelstätter, F., Benke, T., Felber, S., et al. (2006, May). How specifically do we learn? Imaging the learning of multiplication and subtraction. *NeuroImage, 30,* 1365–1375.

Micheloyannis, S., Sakkalis, V., Vourkas, M., Stam, C. J., & Simos, P. G. (2005, January 20). Neural networks involved in mathematical thinking: Evidence from linear and non-linear analysis of electroencephalographic activity. *Neuroscience Letters, 373,* 212–217.

Miller, K., & Paredes, D. R. (1990). Starting to add worse: Effects of learning to multiply on children's addition. *Cognition, 37,* 213–242.

Chapter 6

Barnett, M. A., Quackenbush, S. W., & Sinisi, C. (1996). Factors affecting children's, adolescents', and young adults' perceptions of parental discipline. *Journal of Genetic Psychology, 157*(4), 411–424.

Baron-Cohen, S. (2003). *The essential difference: The truth about the male and female brain.* New York: Basic Books.

Benenson, J. F., & Heath, A. (2006). Boys withdraw more in one-on-one interactions, whereas girls withdraw more in groups. *Developmental Psychology, 42*(2), 272–282.

Buck, G., & Ehlers, N. (2002). Four criteria for engaging girls in the middle level classroom. *Middle School Journal, 34*(1), 48–53.

Carreker, S. (2004). *Dyslexia: Beyond the myth.* Retrieved April 25, 2007, from http://www.ldonline.org/article/277.

Cattaneo, Z., Postma, A., & Vecchi, T. (2006). Gender differences in memory for object and word locations. *Quarterly Journal of Experimental Psychology, 59*(5), 904–919.

de Goede, M., Kessels, R. P. C., & Postma, A. (2006). Individual variation in human spatial ability: Differences between men and women in object location memory. *Cognitive Processing, 7*(Suppl. 1), 153.

Du, Y., Weymouth, C. M., & Dragseth, K. (2003, April 21–25). *Gender differences and student learning.* Paper presented at the annual meeting of the American Educational Research Association, Chicago, IL.

Dysgraphia. (2007). Retrieved April 25, 2007, from http://www.ncld.org/index. php?option=content&task=view&id=468.

Geffen, G., Moar, K. J., Hanlon, A. P., Clark, C. R., & Geffen, L. B. (1990). Performance measures of 16- to 86-year-old males and females on the auditory verbal learning test. *Clinical Neuropsychologist, 4*(1), 45–63.

Geiger, J. F., & Litwiller, R. M. (2005). Spatial working memory and gender differences in science. *Journal of Instructional Psychology, 32*(1), 49–57.

Halpern, D. F. (2000). *Sex differences in cognitive abilities* (3rd ed.). Mahwah, NJ: Lawrence Erlbaum.

Honigsfeld, A., & Dunn, R. (2003). High school male and female learning-style similarities and differences in diverse nations. *The Journal of Educational Research, 96*(4), 195–207.

Horton, N. K., Ray, G. E., & Cohen, R. (2001). Children's evaluations of inductive discipline as a function of transgression type and induction orientation. *Child Study Journal, 31*(2), 71–93.

James, A. N. (2007). *Teaching the male brain: How boys think, feel, and learn in school.* Thousand Oaks, CA: Corwin.

Jones, M. G., Brader-Araje, L., Carboni, L. W., Carter, G., Rua, M. J., Banilower, E., et al. (2000). Tool time: Gender and students' use of tools, control, and authority. *Journal of Research in Science Teaching, 37*(8), 760–783.

Kaufmann, L., Lochy, A., Drexler, A., & Semenza, C. (2004). Deficient arithmetic fact retrieval—storage or access problem? *Neuropsychologia, 42*(4), 482–496.

Kimura, D. (2000). *Sex and cognition.* Cambridge, MA: A Bradford Book/The MIT Press.

Lachance, J. A., & Mazzocco, M. M. M. (2006). A longitudinal analysis of sex differences in math and spatial skills in primary school age children. *Learning & Individual Differences, 16*(3), 195–216.

Lawton, C. A., & Hatcher, D. W. (2005). Gender differences in integration of images in visuospatial memory. *Sex Roles, 53*(9–10), 717–725.

Linderman, J., Kantrowitz, L., & Flannery, K. (2005). Male vulnerability to reading disability is not likely to be a myth: A call for new data. *Journal of Learning Disabilities, 38*(2), 109–129.

Longcamp, M., Boucard, C., Gilhodes, J. C., Anton, J. L., Roth, M., Nazarian, B., et al. (2008). Learning through hand- or typewriting influences visual recognition of new graphic shapes: Behavioral and functional imaging evidence. *Journal of Cognitive Neuroscience, 20*(5), 802–815.

Longcamp, M., Boucard, C., Gilhodes, J. C., & Velay, J. L. (2006). Remembering the orientation of newly learned characters depends on the associated writing knowledge: A comparison between handwriting and typing. *Human Movement Science, 25,* 646–656.

Maccoby, E. E. (1998). *The two sexes: Growing up apart, growing together.* Cambridge, MA: Harvard University Press.

Naglieri, J. A., & Rojahn, J. (2001). Gender differences in planning, attention, simultaneous, and successive (pass) cognitive processes and achievement. *Journal of Educational Psychology, 93*(2), 430–437.

Naka, M. (1998). Repeated writing facilitates children's memory for pseudocharacters and foreign letters. *Memory and Cognition, 26*(4), 804–809.

National Center for Educational Statistics (NCES). (2007). *Percentage of students from kindergarten through eighth grade participating in weekly nonparental afterschool care arrangements: 2005.* Washington, DC: U.S. Department of Education.

Pomerantz, E. M., & Ruble, D. N. (1998). The role of maternal control in the development of sex differences in child self-evaluative factors. *Child Development, 69*(2), 458–478.

Pyryt, M. C., Sandals, L. H., & Begoray, J. (1998). Learning style preferences of gifted, average-ability, and special needs students: A multivariate perspective. *Journal for Research in Childhood Education, 13*(1), 71–76.

Seitsinger, A. M., Barboza, H. C., & Hird, A. (1998, April 13–17). *Single-sex mathematics instruction in an urban independent school.* Paper presented at the annual meeting of the American Educational Research Association, San Diego, CA.

Shalev, R. S. (2004). Developmental dyscalculia. *Journal of Child Neurology, 19*(10), 765–770.

Stumpf, H. (1998). Gender-related differences in academically talented students' scores and use of time on tests of spatial ability. *Gifted Child Quarterly, 42*(3), 157–171.

Tibbetts, S. L. (1977). Sex-role stereotyping and its effects on boys. *Journal of the NAWDAC, 40*(3), 109–111.

Van Houtte, M. (2004). Why boys achieve less at school than girls: The difference between boys' and girls' academic culture. *Educational Studies, 30*(2), 159–173.

Vuontela V., Steenari, M. R., Carlson, S., Koivisto, J., Fjallberg, M., & Aronen, E. T. (2003). Audiospatial and visuospatial working memory in 6–13 year old school children. *Learning and Memory, 10*, 74–81.

Chapter 7

Cage, B., & Smith, J. (2000). The effects of chess instruction on mathematics achievement of southern, rural, black secondary students. *Research in the Schools, 7*(1), 19–26.

Kerns, K. A., McInerney, R. J., & Wilde, N. J. (2001). Time reproduction, working memory, and behavioral inhibition in children with ADHD. *Child Neuropsychology, 7*, 21–31.

Margulies, S. (1991). *The effect of chess on reading scores.* New York: American Chess Federation.

Pereira, A. C., Huddleston, D. E., Brickman, A. M., Sosunov, A. A., Hen, R., McKhann, G. M., et al. (2007). An in vivo correlate of exercise-induced neurogenesis in the adult dentate gyrus. *Proceedings of the National Academy of Sciences of the United States of America, 104*, 5638–5643.

Posner, M., Rothbart, M. K., Sheese, B. E., & Kieras, J. (2008). How arts training influences cognition. In C. Asbury & B. Rich (Eds.), *Learning, arts, and the brain: The Dana Consortium report on arts and cognition* (pp. 1–10). New York: Dana Press.

Westerberg, H., & Klingberg, T. (2007). Changes in cortical activity after training of working memory—A single-subject analysis. *Physiology and Behavior, 92*, 186–192.

Chapter 8

Barr, S. (1997). *Tapestries: Exploring identity and culture in the classroom.* Tucson, AZ: Zephyr Press.

Carter, R. (1998). *Mapping the mind.* London: Weidenfield & Nicholson.

Dispenza, J. (2007). *Evolve your brain.* Deerfield Beach, FL: Health Communications.

Howard, P. (2000). *The owner's manual for the brain* (2nd ed.). Atlanta, GA: Bard Press.

Jensen, E. (2006). *Enriching the brain.* San Francisco: Jossey-Bass.

Kotulak, R. (1997). *Inside the brain*. Kansas City, MO: Andrews McMeel.

Sapolsky, R. (1998). *Why zebras don't get ulcers*. New York: W. H. Freeman.

Chapter 9

Beamon, G. W. (2001). *Teaching with adolescent learning in mind*. Arlington Heights, IL: Skylight Professional Development.

Feinstein, S. (2004). *Secrets of the teenage brain: Research-based strategies for reaching and teaching today's adolescents*. Thousand Oaks, CA: Corwin.

Krepel, W. J., & Duvall, C. R. (1981). *Field trips: A guide for planning and conducting educational experiences*. Washington, DC: National Education Association.

Silver, H., Strong, R., & Perini, M. (2000). *So each may learn: Integrating learning styles and multiple intelligences*. Alexandria, VA: Association for Supervision and Curriculum Development.

Sprenger, M. (2005). *How to teach so students remember*. Alexandria, VA: Association for Supervision and Curriculum Development.

Tate, M. L. (2003). *Worksheets don't grow dendrites: 20 instructional strategies that engage the brain*. Thousand Oaks, CA: Corwin.

Thiers, N. (Ed.). (1995). *Successful strategies: Building a school-to-careers system*. Alexandria, VA: American Vocational Association.

Tileston, D. W. (2004). *What every teacher should know about classroom management and discipline*. Thousand Oaks, CA: Corwin.

U. S. Secretary's Commission on Achieving Necessary Skills. (1991). *What work requires of schools: A SCANS report for America 2000*. Washington, DC: U.S. Department of Labor.

Chapter 10

Budd, J. W. (2004). Mind maps as classroom exercises. *Journal of Economic Education, 35*(1), 35–46.

Coggins, D., Kravin, D., Coates, G. D., & Carrol, M. D. (2007). *English language learners in the mathematics classroom*. Thousand Oaks, CA: Corwin.

Deshler, D., & Schmaker, J. (2006). *Teaching adolescents with disabilities: Accessing the general education curriculum*. Thousand Oaks, CA: Corwin.

Feinstein, S. (2004). *Secrets of the teenage brain: Research-based strategies for reaching and teaching today's adolescents*. Thousand Oaks, CA: Corwin.

Goldberg, C. (2004). Brain friendly techniques: Mind mapping. *School Library Media Activities Monthly, 21*(3), 22–24.

Gregory, G. H., & Parry, T. (2006). *Designing brain-compatible learning* (3rd ed.). Thousand Oaks, CA: Corwin.

Jensen, E. (2007). *Brain-compatible strategies* (2nd ed.). Victoria Australia: Hawker Brownlow Education.

Marzano, R. J. (2007). *The art and science of teaching*. Alexandria, VA: Association for Supervision and Curriculum Development.

Posamentier, A. S., & Jaye, D. (2006). *What successful math teachers do, Grades 6–12: 79 research-based strategies for the standards-based classroom*. Thousand Oaks, CA: Corwin.

Ronis, D. L. (2006). *Brain-compatible mathematics* (2nd ed.). Thousand Oaks, CA: Corwin.

Sousa, D. A. (2007). *How the special needs brain learns* (2nd ed.). Thousand Oaks CA: Corwin.

CORWIN
A SAGE Company

The Corwin logo—a raven striding across an open book—represents the union of courage and learning. Corwin is committed to improving education for all learners by publishing books and other professional development resources for those serving the field of PreK–12 education. By providing practical, hands-on materials, Corwin continues to carry out the promise of its motto: **"Helping Educators Do Their Work Better."**